She was no Lady

She was no Lady

◆

A personal journey of recovery through Hurricane Katrina

Michael Tracey

iUniverse, Inc.
New York Lincoln Shanghai

She was no Lady
A personal journey of recovery through Hurricane Katrina

Copyright © 2006 by Michael Tracey

All rights reserved. No part of this book may be used or reproduced by any means, graphic, electronic, or mechanical, including photocopying, recording, taping or by any information storage retrieval system without the written permission of the publisher except in the case of brief quotations embodied in critical articles and reviews.

iUniverse books may be ordered through booksellers or by contacting:

iUniverse
2021 Pine Lake Road, Suite 100
Lincoln, NE 68512
www.iuniverse.com
1-800-Authors (1-800-288-4677)

ISBN-13: 978-0-595-39079-3 (pbk)
ISBN-13: 978-0-595-83468-6 (ebk)
ISBN-10: 0-595-39079-X (pbk)
ISBN-10: 0-595-83468-X (ebk)

Printed in the United States of America

Dedicated to Jo Sharp, our faithful, loyal and committed secretary who continues to grow strong in the broken places of her life, following Hurricane Katrina

Contents

Preface		ix
CHAPTER 1	It's Vacation Time Again	1
CHAPTER 2	Welcome to Katrina's Hell	11
CHAPTER 3	Give Me a Call	19
CHAPTER 4	The Suitcase Priest	23
CHAPTER 5	Get Me to the Church	29
CHAPTER 6	What Do We Do Now?	34
CHAPTER 7	"How Are You Doing?"	42
CHAPTER 8	Reconnecting	50
CHAPTER 9	What Do You Say?	65
CHAPTER 10	You Say, "I do."	79
CHAPTER 11	When Will It Be Rebuilt?	88
CHAPTER 12	It Is Thanksgiving Again!	91
CHAPTER 13	It's Just a Simple Christmas	97
CHAPTER 14	Restless Days and Restless Nights	104
CHAPTER 15	Inconclusive Conclusions	110
CHAPTER 16	Healing Postscripts	113

Preface

○ ○

I walked a mile with Pleasure, she chatted all the way.
But left me none the wiser for all she had to say.
I walked a mile with Sorrow, not a word said she.
But, oh, the things I learned when sorrow walked with me.

—-Robert Browning Hamilton

Since the arrival and total devastation caused by Hurricane Katrina on August 29, 2005, I have walked several miles with Sorrow.

As I walked with her, I mourned my losses—my home, my personal belongings, my car, my comfort zone, my security, my routine, my plans for the future, and my normality.

She has taught me many things. She has been a companion and a friend; a questioner and an informer; a humbler and a challenger; a faith tester and a doubt prober; a hope builder and a despairing thorn in the side.

She has made me a believer in people's goodness as well as their fragility in the midst of great catastrophes; a believer in miracles, no matter how small, as well as the depths of despair that can haunt; a believer in the gift of faith as well as how fickle it can be when tested; a believer in the gift of hope as well as the pits of hopelessness that can ensnare; a believer in oceans of love and mountains of support as well as the loneliness that often paralyzes the lost.

We often complain about our routine, our comfort zone, our schedule being interrupted by people who just happen to drop in. We complain about events we don't plan and schedules we don't make, that surprise us. We complain about all the disruptions in our lives, as small as an unplanned phone call or as big as a visit from a hurricane. What we fail to realize is that the interruptions are not so much interruptions as such, but life itself opening up before us; making us realize we cannot control its coming and goings but we can control how we embrace it. We have a choice.

The poet, Rainer Marie Rilke, asks us to "Be patient toward all that is unsolved in your heart and try to love the questions themselves. Live the question now. Perhaps then, gradually, without knowing it, live along some distant day into the answer."

We try to get rid of the pain by being busy, being preoccupied; we want someone to listen, to notice us, to feel our pain. We like easy, painless victories; maybe, hoping to wake up some day and discover that Hurricane Katrina was just a horrible dream. We want growth without crisis; healing without pain and resurrection without a cross.

We know that elegant phrases or lofty thoughts do not soothe the pain. They ring hollow. When we learn to move through our suffering rather than to avoid it, then maybe it has a better chance of teaching us. We face our losses, we grieve them; maybe they have imprisoned us and kept us in denial. We have to face our wounds, just like a dog licks his wounds with his curative tongue. We can spend our life thinking about what happened to us in the hurricane or we can ask ourselves how can we live though this and discover what it is trying to tell us. We have a choice: we can drown in the losses or we can choose to live through them. One is escape; the other has growth potential.

This book is my journey; a journey from many questions to some answers; from much pain to some healing; from much anger to some acceptance; from much chaos to some order; from much testing to some renewal; from much fear to some trust; from much sorrow to some peace.

I use the word "some" in areas of growth because it is a journey, a process, an ongoing adventure. Each day brings new challenges that will bring new growth eventually.

Perhaps, nature has been my best encourager. Initially, the trees, remaining following Hurricane Katrina, were in shock. They were confused, not knowing their season. Gradually, they rediscovered their identity and their cycle. I, too, was shocked and confused initially, not knowing my true self. Gradually, I came home to myself and continued on the journey of recovery, discovery and wholeness.

Parker J. Parker, in his book, "A Hidden Wholeness : The Journey Toward an Undivided Life," reminds me that "Wholeness does not mean perfection. It means embracing brokenness as an integral part of life. Knowing this gives me hope that human wholeness—mine, yours, ours—need not be a utopian dream, if we can use devastation as a seedbed for new life."

New seeds have to die in the dark bowels of the earth before they can usher in a new season, a new spring. Perhaps the devastation caused by Hurricane Katrina brought us deeper into our own individual sanctums in order to make all things new again.

1

It's Vacation Time Again

I say "goodbye" to the parishioners of Our Lady of the Gulf Church in Bay St. Louis on a Sunday morning in late July 2005. I remind them not to expect me to worry about them while I am away. I tell them not to expect me to think of them suffering in the humid days while I bask in cool temperature where "humidity" is not in the dictionary. I remind them that I will not worry about them even in the middle of the hurricane, I assure then that I will not be calling long-distance every few days to check on how things are going. After all, I will be on vacation.

I sign enough checks for Jo, our parish secretary; give her an emergency phone number in Ireland as well as an email address. I have answered all her questions and I am ready for vacation.

I give Jim, our maintenance person, some quotes for our parish sign while I am away. It is ironic that the last one I give him becomes providential.

I am ready for a well-earned vacation, away from the hot, humid days of summer. I will not have to worry about any funeral, wedding, baptism or appointment for a month. I know that when the phone rings at my family home in Ireland, no one will be calling me. I am no longer "on call," "on duty." I am on vacation.

The Delta jet speeds across the night sky, filled with passengers, ready for a vacation; a business meeting; a planned escape; a few days of golfing; a visit with family and friends. As I settle down in seat 27G—a window seat, I hope I do not have a chatty neighbor. I need some time to relax and I hope to rest my weary eyes on the long flight.

Seven hours later, I am ready to touchdown in Ireland. I go through the formality of passport control, Customs and exit to meet my waiting family. I reconnect with them again as I catch up on all the local news and gossip since last time. Slowly, we make our way to a boyhood home. Here, I am at home again, at home with myself, my roots and my family. Now, I am my own boss again. I can go to bed when I want, get up when I want and even eat what I want without the consequences of gaining weight. After all, I have been blessed with good metabolism.

Now, I have a chance to stay up late into the early morning and rise in the late morning. I don't have to be anywhere; meet anyone or do anything. After all, I am on vacation.

Vacation time is a time when you hope time will stand still and you can savor each moment without deadlines or schedules, without pressure or performance; without appointments or appendage. It is a time to recharge body and battle weary bones; a time to catch up on local events and local people; to reconnect with storied characters and wise counselors.

On occasions, I glance at the evening news to discover if there are any dramatic news stories happening around the world. I find out that I do not have to worry about anything happening elsewhere. After all, I am on vacation. I am in my own world, insulated and isolated but happy.

A cursory glance at the evening news in late August captured my attention. It stated that a hurricane had entered the Gulf of Mexico. It was called Hurricane Katrina. I found the name interesting because I had a niece called Caitriona. Somehow, the name became implanted in my brain. Little did I know that, she was to have a profound effect on my life and my world.

Living on the Mississippi Gulf Coast allowed me to become educated on the power and scope of hurricanes. I became fascinated with their formation, their pattern as well as their non-sexist names. I plodded their progress through "The Weather Channel." I checked the coordinates on a hurricane map supplied by the local newspaper. I watched computer models and possible paths they might take toward their final destination. I listened to people make plans if one of them might ever strike our area. The people always measured life in terms of BC and AC "Before Camille" and "After Camille." Hurricane Camille in August 1969 became the benchmark for all future hurricanes. I listened to stories of recovery and bravery; stories of neighbor helping neighbor; stories of organized chaos and long-term rebuilding. I put all those thoughts and stories aside. After all, I was on vacation and I needed to enjoy it.

As the days went on, the projected path of Hurricane Katrina became more speculative. It could strike anywhere from the Florida Panhandle to Texas. Obviously, I didn't have to worry, it is not going to hit Mississippi. After all, I am on vacation and I should not let anything distract me from enjoying it.

I busy myself relaxing and enjoying roaming around the countryside of my boyhood. Occasionally, I glance at the news headlines. Scant references to a hurricane possibly threatening the Gulf Coast continue to surface. The reports catch my attention. Now, I am more than curious. I am really interested—at least, from a distance.

Some days later, the news reports worry me. Indications are that Hurricane Katrina will hit the Mississippi Gulf Coast. I fear the worst and hope for the best.

My sisters, Ann and Eileen, call from England. They, too, have heard about the possible path of the hurricane. They look for some assurance and information. I remind them that we have to wait and see what will happen during the next few days.

During the next few days, I pay closer attention to every newscast, trying to find out what might happen to my adopted state some 4,000 miles away. Desperately, I want to know what is happening; what the prognosis might be as well as the implication for me.

On Sunday evening, August 28th, 2005, I receive an email that would change the rest of my life. Jo, our parish secretary, emailed me to say that her family were leaving for Panama City, Florida. The inevitable would happen. She indicated that Hurricane Katrina was slated to come ashore just west of Bay St. Louis; that most people were leaving the area and everyone was asked to evacuate. She indicated that they had taken the Blessed Sacrament from Our Lady of the Gulf Church and brought it to nearby St. Stanislaus chapel on the second floor of the campus. They had unplugged all the computers and turned off the air conditioning at the parish offices and said goodbye to the parish and area.

My heart began to sink in anticipation of the possible destruction that Katrina could cause to our town of Bay St. Louis with its motto of "A Place Apart." I feared that it might become "a place torn apart." All I could do was wait and hope.

On Tuesday, August 30, 2005 at 14:07 hours, I received an email from Jo. It simply read: "We are in Panama City at the Beachbreak by the Sea. My sister and her family came too. We cannot get in touch with anyone in Slidell, Bay St. Louis, or elsewhere. According to the news, things are not at all good. WLOX TV report states that all of downtown Bay St. Louis is 'destroyed.' One CNN reporter said an elderly couple floated down DeMontluzin Avenue and made it into a house. We have absolutely no idea what is left. We cannot reach a soul. I do not know if my mother and stepfather are okay or not. Please, please, please pray for everyone. We don't know when we can go home. We are very scared but grateful to be here. The Ocean Springs bridge is gone; the Bay St. Louis bridge is gone; St. Thomas is gone; the President Casino is in the parking lot of the Coliseum. New Orleans is of course a mess. But Waveland, Bay St. Louis, Pass Christian, Long Beach, Gulfport, etc. took the brunt of it and it is not pretty. I do not know if you will be able to fly in. we will try to check back our email to see if you respond. Again, please pray for everyone. We all love you and will try to reach you soon. Peace, Jo."

Once I read the email and printed it, I shared it with my family. I needed space. I walked down a country lane, away from anyone, carrying a bucketful of questions, fears and uncertainties. I tried to fight back the tears and be brave but they would not cooperate. I needed space as my mind flooded with "what now?" questions. I was so far away; felt so helpless; paralyzed by a reality I could only look at from afar. After the long walk, I tried to distract myself to no avail. I tried to be busy about other things but only one thing continued to grab my focus.

Later that night, I got a phone from Jo. Amid the tears, she confirmed all she had shared in her earlier email. She kept saying, "It's bad. It's real bad. There is nothing left. The church is badly damaged. We don't know how bad. The rectory is gone. There is nothing left." My silence affirmed my stunned feelings. I was devastated, without even being there.

Later on, my sisters called from England. They looked for the latest news and information. I told them. They were shocked. Their questions were the same: "What are you going to do?" I knew one thing I was going to do. Everything else was in limbo.

During the next few days, I scrutinized all the newscasts to try and ascertain the extent of the damage. Jo, our parish secretary, kept in touch and called several times with updates. Good friends, Bill and Carolyn, emailed me an aerial view of the destroyed Beach Blvd., near downtown Bay St. Louis. Like a homicide detective, I poured over all the details in the picture. What once were familiar landmarks along the beach were barely recognizable. The area resembled a charred landscape after a raging fire. Blackened and bare stumps of mangled trees stood like scarecrows, twisted and torn by a cruel fate. I searched for a home that no longer existed; a church that, at least, outwardly, still stood as a reminder of the eternal. Reality came knocking on the door of my heart and I had no choice but to let it in with its hellish destruction and desolation.

Nightly, my sisters called. They looked for updates. They shared what they had viewed on TV there. My sister, Eileen, continued to ask, "What are you going to do?" Deep down, I knew what I was going to do. I didn't know the "how." I did know it would be painful. How painful? I am still finding out.

Consistently, night after night, my sister, Eileen, called and asked that same question—what are you going to do? "I'm going back!" I answered her. Even though she was a sister, her mothering instinct came through. "You should think seriously of not going back. What do you have to go back to?" she asked. "Why don't you wait for a few weeks until things improve? You might get sick and then you will be no good to yourself or to anyone else."

I listened intently; appreciated her concern but I had made up my mind. I was going back. I needed to go back to Bay St. Louis. I needed to be with the people. I needed to listen to their stories, their hurts, their angers, their confusion and even their despair. I had invested my life in their lives and now, I had no choice but to continue that investment.

I was scheduled to return to Bay St. Louis on Friday, September 2nd. But I had a major problem. Could I get to Bay St. Louis? I check Delta airlines web site. Obviously, I encounter the first roadblocks. New Orleans, Gulfport and Mobile airports are closed. Delta indicates that, if one is scheduled to fly into any of the above airports, one can change without penalty, provided one flies by September 6th. I call Delta airlines and reschedule my flight into Gulfport for September 6th. Obviously, I hope that Gulfport airport will be open by then.

On Saturday evening, my sister, Eileen, calls again and says, "You must watch the BBC evening news this evening. I think I saw a picture of your church on it." I wait and watch the 10 p.m. BBC Evening News. Obviously, the lead story is "Hurricane Katrina." The camera pans along the beach in Bay St. Louis and gradually zooms up to a clock. The face of the clock reads, "4:50 a.m." The reporter begins, "This is when time stood still, when Hurricane Katrina came ashore here. This moment is frozen in time forever."

The rest of the newscast didn't matter. Now, we knew. Time stood still and, as a family, we stood still to ponder that frozen moment. In my own silence, I wondered and agonized over how I would unfreeze that time again.

Visitors came and went. I knew they were there but, somehow, I was not connected with them. I was connected long distance with another place, I called "home."

The remaining days of my extended vacation were, not only filled with questions, but also trying to discern ways I could even help from afar. We started an emergency Hurricane Katrina Fund at a local bank. Then, the publicity began. We set up interviews on some local radio programs, with newspapers and the evening news shows.

Further calls from Jo, our parish secretary, confirmed our worst fears. "The rectory is gone, completely destroyed," she indicated. Kathleen, our Pastoral Associate, called. She affirmed everything. She and her family had braved the hurricane and stayed at home. They regretted the decision and had to climb on top of furniture to escape the surging waters. Then, they left the area.

Usually, when I go on vacation, I bring at least two pieces of luggage. Of course, some of the items packed are gifts for family. On my return trips, my luggage is a lot lighter—one piece of luggage within another and I can whiz through airports. This time, it was going to be different and my sister, Bernie, knew it.

She arrived that evening with a supply of things she felt I might need in the immediate future when I returned. She purchased some T-shirts, jeans, shirts, toiletries, towels, snack items, gloves. Obviously, I would return to the States with two filled pieces of luggage.

I preached at weekend Masses at churches in the area; reminding them of the devastation that visited the Bay St. Louis and surrounding areas. They were stunned. Devastation such as this impacted them. No longer did this disaster visit some unknown place in a foreign country. It visited the home town of someone they knew and grew up with. They responded.

On Sunday night, my mind allowed me to go to bed and sleep. All of a sudden, there was a knock on the door. My nephew reminded me that there was "some woman from Mississippi on the phone and wants to talk to me." I donned some clothes and headed for the phone. It was Mary Ann. She apologized for waking me. She was so excited to hear my voice. She talked so fast that she was like someone trying to break a world record as they sprinted to the finish line.

Once she finished apologizing, she updated me on what was happening. Then, she asked me a surprising and puzzling question, "Seeing what you have seen about the hurricane and all the destruction it has caused; do you still want to come back to us?" Her voice began to quiver with emotion and I could sense that tears were on the horizon. I responded, "Of course, I am coming back." Excitedly, she asked, "You are?" "Yes, I am." She went on to offer me a place at her business in Gulfport. I took her phone number, thanked her and told her I would be in touch soon.

Early on Monday morning, I drove through the fog to the local radio station for a live interview with one of the top rated presenters in the country. The twenty minute interview went well. I shared the information I had received; indicated some of the anticipated situations I would face on my return and, of course, I reminded the listeners how they could help by contributing to the emergency fund we had set up at a local bank.

As soon as I left the radio stations, the cell phone began to ring. Already, people were calling, saying how they were going to help. When I finally got home, more phone calls awaited me. I felt overwhelmed by the outpouring of support.

In the meantime, I deliberated on how I might be able to get back to my parish in Bay St. Louis. Some family friends, living in Atlanta, offered me a place with them until I could make my way to the Mississippi Gulf Coast. As time went on, a priest friend living in Jackson, offered me a base there as a stepping stone to get to the Gulf Coast.

On Monday afternoon, I checked the Delta Airlines web site again to find about the status of airports I might possibly fly into. Gulfport airport remained closed. The only alternative was to fly into the nearest open airport—Mobile. I called Delta and changed my flight. I would fly into Mobile.

Later that afternoon, I called Mary Ann and left a message indicating that I would be flying into Mobile. I hoped they would be able to pick me up at the airport.

My mind jumped ahead. What about celebrating Mass when I go back? Will there be any vestments or have they all been washed away by the hurricane? What about other supplies? The local Apostolic Work Center in the nearby town calls and offers vestments and other supplies. I accept their generous offer of sets of vestments, albs, altar linens, chalice and other items. Briege and her staff overwhelm me with their generosity. They even give me a tour of their facility where they make all kinds of church supplies for parishes, especially for the missions.

I needed to finalize some things before my flight the next morning. First of all, I needed a tetanus shot. While I waited in the doctor's office, the local news was being broadcast. There in the middle of the newscast, I heard my voice and for the next 5 minutes listened to the telephone interview I did earlier with the news director. Once again, it brought forth emotions that were to become commonplace during the next few months. As I watched the others in the waiting room, I wondered about them. They were concerned about their own aches and pains while I was concerned with a pain that could not be cured by a simple visit to a doctor's clinic.

Following the doctor's visit, I do some last minute shopping. Some packages of soup are top of the menu. They are easy to carry, quick to fix and nourishing. I also grab some cookies to munch on during some of the quiet moments I anticipate having during the next few days.

On returning home, I noticed an elderly gentleman waiting for me. He is in his late 70's and had driven thirty miles to meet me. He heard my interview on the radio early that morning as he was driving to the market with some lambs he had for sale. He sold his lambs at the market. He then took the check he received in payment, went into the local bank, cashed it, changed the Euros into Dollars and came to see me and give it to me to help the people. I was speechless at this tremendous gesture of generosity.

As the evening and night wore on, neighbors and friends arrived with contributions to the emergency fund for our parish. They had gone to the trouble of converting their Euros into dollars. I was overwhelmed by their generosity. At the same time, their gifts reminded me of what I would face when I returned to Mississippi the following day.

That night, I got little sleep. My mind wandered to a desperate situation I had heard about days earlier. I had seen the pictures on TV; read the news reports; read the emails from friends there. But, still, I was 4,000 miles away, still untouched by the depth and scope of the devastation.

During the night, I twist and turn. My mind is filled with questions with no readymade answers. All, I know was that I need to get back and do "something." I do not know what that "something" might be or whether or not I will have the resources and inner strength to do it. Sooner or later, I would find out as well as its cost, both physically, emotionally and spiritually.

I arrive at Shannon airport early the next morning. My body is still in Ireland but my mind is thousands of miles away. I go through the routine of checking in and go upstairs to the departure lounge. It contains the Duty Free Shop. I browse around it, not really looking for anything to purchase but just as a distraction from the fear, tears and trials I anticipate ahead. I pass through the Immigration Checkpoint and eventually board Delta Flight 129, non-stop to Atlanta, continuing on to Mobile and beyond. I find my window seat—25G; put away my laptop and carryon bag and settle into the seat for the next eight hours. I hope and pray that I will not be visited by a chatty neighbor who will entertain me for the journey. I just want to be left alone; left to my own thoughts as I try to visualize and imagine what is ahead. The more I think about it, the more I have to fight back the tears. Dinner is served later and that distracts me from the pain and troubling thoughts. I munch on chicken that easily falls apart as I slice it with the white plastic knife. I wish my thoughts and fears could be dissected as easily. I try to settle down and close my eyes. My body is tired but my mind races ahead. I put on the earphones, hoping that some music channel might lull me to sleep or distract me from my torturous thoughts. I don't even bother to check the movie that is playing. I glance at it occasionally without its audio. I don't even know the name of the movie and I really don't care.

Finally, we land in Atlanta. I negotiate the underground and get to the departure gate where I will board a flight to Mobile. I count down the hours and minutes by walking up and down the long corridors, pausing now and then to drop into a store to browse. The distractions help for a while. Eventually, I sit down by the departure gate and just watch the travelers rush by. I try to imagine where they are going. Is it business or pleasure? Is their trip filled with reunion or departure? Are they going home or leaving? What emotions do they carry within those fast-paced bodies? Do they have the time to listen to their innermost thoughts? I do and I wish they were not so muddled and painful.

On arriving at Mobile as the evening begins its journey of turning day into night, I watch the people exiting, reuniting and rushing off into the darkening outsides. I glance around, looking for some familiar faces who are supposed to pick me up at the airport. Soon, the airport is quiet. There are no more flights to arrive; no more passengers to welcome for the rest of the evening. I still wait and wonder. I wonder if Mike and Mary Ann got my message that I would be flying into Mobile and asking them to pick me up at the airport. I still have her cell phone number. Maybe, I could call her to find out. All the phones seem to be in use. So I wait.

Eventually, someone rushes in through the sliding door. She looks familiar. It is her. I recognize that excited smile. We hug and my heart beat returns to normal. Mike, her husband and Laurie, their daughter, follow close behind. I pick up my suitcases and follow them to their company pickup truck. As I am about to put my luggage into the open bed of the truck, Mike reminded me not to put it in. "It is probably contaminated," he says. That word sets off a whole stream of emotions and fears. Another dose of anticipated reality begins to be realized.

When we get in the truck, they mention how bad the traffic was and that was why they were late. We make small talk about my trip and if I enjoyed it. I told them I enjoyed it up until a lady named Katrina destroyed it. They are careful not to speak too much about what I might see in my home town. They want me to discover it for myself. They mention about a meeting at the Diocesan Offices in the morning for priests to update them on the situation and some steps to take.

My friends stop at the drive-thru of a hamburger place to pick up their supper. They ask me if I want anything to eat. I don't. My mind is filled and my body doesn't even want to think of hunger. They order their hamburgers and we head toward the Interstate, while they munch on their burgers and make comments about how they taste. I just sit in the back with Laurie, sandwiched between two suitcases.

Through the darkening landscape, I can see automobiles abandoned along the Interstate. I am told that people left them there when they ran out of gas. Another outline piece of the devastating puzzle clicked into place. As we travel toward Mississippi, I notice snapped pine trees, another sign of a cruel visitor. We press on and encounter a section of the bridge destroyed. We make the detour and continue through the starless sky to a place I will call "home" for the next few months.

Finally, we arrive at Mike and Mary Ann's business, just off the Interstate in Gulfport. This is my first time here but it will become a familiar and loving place for a long time. Other members of her family are also staying there. Just off the front office, there is a large room strewn with air mattresses. Salvaged personal clothing is neatly folded on a nearby table. Mary Ann shows me my air mattress on the floor in the corner. She says, "You know we love you. You are one of the family. You can come and go as you wish."

Shortly afterwards, I excuse myself and collapse onto my air mattress. The family members stay and visit. Soon, I was asleep, totally exhausted both mentally and physically.

Some days later, Mary Ann hands me some photos she had taken. She said they include a photo of me. I looked through the photos and saw the one she mentioned. I just looked at her and smiled. She had taken a photo of me sleeping on my air mattress that first night. "You just looked like you were dead. You had your hands crossed over your chest and you were out of it." Yes, I was "out of it." I may have looked like I was "dead." But I was still breathing and I needed every breath to face the demolition derby that Katrina created.

I am spending my first night back in Mississippi, lying on an air mattress, realizing that the worst is yet to come.

2

Welcome to Katrina's Hell

The next morning, jet lag kicks in and I am awake early. I'm not sure what time it is. I feel for my watch to check but it is too dark to read the time. I don't want to get up in the dark and disturb the others so I lie there in my own thoughts and unanswered questions. Eventually, others begin to stir and a new day begins. I dress in the same clothes I arrived in and face the unknown.

The business is blessed to have power and a shower; a kitchen and some breakfast food. Most of all, it is blessed with very generous and caring people who will carry each other through the purgatory and recovery.

Now, I am beginning to realize what it is like to be interdependent rather than independent; to be on the receiving end rather than on the giving end; to be human rather than feeling the need to be strong.

I go through the motion of eating breakfast. I don't even remember what I ate. Maybe I had a cup of tea and some cinnamon rolls. Obviously, I didn't have coffee because it is not my cup of tea.

Mary Ann drives me to Biloxi to the morning meeting with the other priests of the diocese and the bishop. As I enter the meeting, I notice that few priests are wearing clerical black. This is another sign of personal loss. Fellow priests, in somber moods, greet each other. There is no excitement in the air. Instead there is an unspoken solidarity which would prove to be a lifeline in the coming months. The bishop arrives, clutching a cup of coffee in a paper cup. He sports an open-necked black shirt with short sleeves and no jacket. Carpet has been torn from the floor and the acoustical tile on the ceiling is missing in many places. The bishop calls the meeting to order and begins with a prayer, asking for guidance, support, strength and courage from God in the days and months ahead.

The agenda for the meeting is set. The bishop makes some opening factual remarks about the status of properties. 10 of 28 churches in the diocese are usable; 68 of the 82 counties have been declared disaster areas. He outlines a fourfold purpose for the meeting. Firstly, we will discover some of the resources available; secondly, we will get information on some financial questions; thirdly, we will discuss some immediate and needed repairs and finally, we will talk about the welfare of the priests during this disaster.

I jot down some notes as he speaks but my mind has moved west to a difference place. When the bishop speaks about the welfare of the priests, I listen intently and wonder how realistic such advice might be. He mentions that we will be called upon to do grief counseling for our parishioners; that we need to take care of ourselves and one another; that we need to pace ourselves; look for the positive; don't let survivor's guilt get to us and use our spirituality to give us and others hope.

I listen to reports on the status of parish properties. St. Michael's Church, Rectory and Parish Hall in Biloxi have been completely destroyed. St Thomas Church, School, Rectory and Parish Center in Long Beach has been completely destroyed. The same fate visited St. Paul's parish in Pass Christian and St. Clare's parish in Waveland. I wait to hear the report on Our Lady of the Gulf parish in Bay St. Louis—my home parish. The report: the church received extensive damage. Soon, reality would give me the real answer.

The mood is somber among the priests as everyone tries to put on a brave front; tries to dig deep and be strong for their parishioners even though they are falling apart emotionally inside themselves. I have yet to visit my destroyed parish.

I call my Congressman's office to see if there is a chance of getting a trailer so I can set up a presence in my parish. He is also a parishioner and has lost his home as well. It seems Katrina did not discriminate. I am told it may be weeks before I can get a trailer to use as a base to help my parishioners reconstruct their lives.

As I ride with Mary Ann down Interstate 10 to my parish of Our Lady of the Gulf in Bay St. Louis, Mississippi, some 30 miles away, I notice the trees, crumbled like broken match sticks that are strewn along the interstate. Cars dot the roadside, mostly having run out of gas; others are twisted and mangled, resembling a junk car cemetery. As Mary Ann, her daughter, Laurie, who just started college, gets closer to Bay St. Louis, an eerie and quiet feeling envelops us. Very little is said as we gaze off into the distance and dwell on our own unanswered questions and thoughts.

Finally, we arrive in the city. We stop off at the home of our parish sacristan, Ethel, who is in her late 70's. I find her inside, lying on an army cot, trying to get some sleep. She is disoriented. As she tells me about the destruction, tears come easily, "what are we going to do?" she asks, knowing that I do not have a magical answer. Mary Ann drops me off at what used to be our rectory and heads to her own home in the area to see if she can find anything that can be salvaged. I stand there in my own thoughts amid the piles of brick, twisted metal, dangling electrical wires, 2 X 4 studs and I glance through the building to the calm Gulf of Mexico. Armed with a pair of boots, a pair of surgical gloves and a few bottles of water, I stand there, dumbfounded in the 95 degree heat. I don't know what to feel anymore. There is anger at the loss of years of personal possessions. A place I called home for the past five years now throws me onto the street. A place that contained my support network now stripped me naked. There are thoughts and wonderment about the future.

This place was special, I tell myself. I notice that I am now using the past tense. I started off my priesthood here in Bay St. Louis in 1972 and spent four special years here. I measured all other assignments, using this one as a measuring rod. The rectory was built in 1971 and claimed to be "hurricane proof." Obviously, a lady called "Katrina" had other plans.

I stand there as if hypnotized, afraid to move. There are no people around. I am glad. I am in no mood to talk to anyone. I just need my own space to try and begin to unscramble my own thoughts and feelings.

I glance at the surrounding buildings as my eyes wanders around the complex. I still cannot move but I need to move. I cannot stay like this forever. I need to do something, just anything to shake off this paralysis.

Some time later, I slowly make my way through the crumbled rectory. At least the carport is standing so I will have some shade from the blistering heat. Negotiating the broken glass, shattered dishes, splintered timbers, dangling electrical wires, occasional piece of cutlery and sanitary ware, I search, not knowing for what but somehow compelled to. Gingerly, I make my way up to the front of the rectory where once the parish offices stood. I try to visualize each office and where things were. My office, which once gave me a pristine view of the Gulf of Mexico, has disappeared into oblivion or into that same Gulf of Mexico. I walk through the office slab. There is nothing. The carpet is wrestled away to lay bare the concrete. The walls and windows are non existent. The entire book-shelved wall that houses my thirty-three year collection of books is just a memory. A computer that once sat on a desk where I penned all my articles and research lay bludgeoned to death by cruel fate somewhere.

I stand in the open spaces for a long time, glancing down at the clean swept floor and stealing glances at a serene Gulf of Mexico across the street. My thoughts become unchristian and my anger diabolic. I don't apologize. I have to be honest with my feelings, recognize them and maybe, some day, move beyond them to healing, hope and rebuilding.

I walk through the sand strewn parking lot to the Church. The doors are unlocked. In fact, they are not there—any of them. Outside, the brickwork looks fine. Earlier this year, we had just finished weatherproofing the church, putting in new air conditioning and heating; painting the walls; resurfacing the floors; refinishing the pews; putting on new roofs; refurbishing the pipe organ. Now, I am to discover the real wrath of Katrina.

Part of the main roof stands naked against the blue sky. Her support beams lie thrashed on the ground nearby. I look for the main eighteen foot doors that stood as sentries against the cruel sea for so long. Now they have given up the ghost. I notice that they are carried by Mother Nature's fury to the inner sanctuary. So much for holy doors, I think. I stand in the aisle at the back where brides stand momentarily before they take the long walk down the aisle into the arms of a waiting husband to be and live happily ever afterward. But today is no fairytale romance. It is a cruel irony. My eyes ponder an empty church, save a few sturdy pews that stood stubbornly against the tide. The rest, broken in pieces, were cascaded into the Gulf of Mexico. I see the two angels who stood guard at the entrance transplanted to the sanctuary area. As I look around at the stained glass windows, I notice one, in particular is badly damaged. It is "The Assumption of Mary into Heaven." I think to myself that we will need lots of miracles to lift us up from this catastrophe. "Where is the ornate Communion rail that graced the sanctuary area, a reminder of part of our history?" It, too, lies in shambles, strewn around the sanctuary. At least, the altar looks intact, I notice. It reminds me of power and strength from another source and we will need a lifetime of such in the weeks and months ahead.

As I walk around the debris covered floor, I notice that the floor is buckled as if hit by a miniature earthquake. It seems the sand, silt, debris and water that washed into the basement, caused the floor to buckle.

I just stand there in the silence. I think of all the work and effort we generated to make our spiritual home elegant again; all the sacrifices parishioners and patrons made to make the grand lady of our city, grand again. Now, we have to start all over again. I don't like the thoughts that flood my mind but I know they are natural and I should not be ashamed of them or apologize for them.

I look at the paintings on the ceiling. They seem okay. Yet, I see daylight streaming down between the panels. I hope it doesn't rain. If it does, our paintings will be destroyed.

I examine the water mark in the church. It too, like water marks in people's homes, becomes a watershed in people's stories and memories.

I travel up into the sanctuary amid the broken pieces of pews, the shattered pieces of marble and the water soaked carpet that once wore its majestic blue so proudly. In the sacristy, I find a place ravaged and pillaged by wind and water. Sacred books lie on the ground, soaked in mold and moisture. I open a closet where once stood regal vestments of various colors. Now, they support that "damn spot" that even Lady Macbeth could not wash out.

I walk outside again to the once proud Beach Boulevard. It now resembles a dirt road leading to a dead end. I glance back at the Lady. I am both proud of her and, at the same time, sad for her. She whispers, "I will recover." I hope and pray that I will have the strength, wisdom and resources to help her in that recovery process.

I walk slowly and sporadically around the rest of the church and some more of the parish property. Minutes later, I turn back. I have seen enough for now. I need to digest and process all this. I need time and space.

I return to what used to be the rectory. I find an old beat up metal chair and sit on it in the shade afforded by the still surviving carport. I bury my head in my hands. My heart is heavy and my mental anguish is overwhelming. I just sit there for a long time as if my feet were nailed to the concrete. I am immune to any traffic that may pass by and wonder about this forlorn figure sitting among the rubble. Frequently, army helicopters buzz overhead, ferrying troops and military police. Occasionally, an army jeep passes by, slows down, and asks if I need some water or food. I simply shake my head.

Eventually, I shake off the paralysis. I get up and begin to move again as I open a bottle of now lukewarm water. It still tastes good as it tries to douse the flames of pain within.

I decide to take my digital camera and snap some pictures of the destruction. I know I want to document the catastrophe for myself and maybe others. As I shoot pictures of all the destruction, I realize something very profound. I have donned another hat. I am distancing myself from the destruction. I am becoming an observer rather than a participant. I know I need more time to not only face the reality but also to participate in it.

Over sixty pictures later, I decide to put down my camera and gingerly walk through the ruins. Like an acrobat on a tightrope, I slowly but methodically make my way through the ruins of what used to be home. Broken glass, battered bricks, electrical conduit and twisted metal slow my progress. I am not sure why I am doing this. But I know I have to do this. Maybe, I am doing it because I need to face the obvious. Maybe, there is an innate hope that I might find something of value which would connect me with the past. The many maybes become wishes that are quickly tempered by a dose of reality.

Momentarily, I marvel at discovering a dish or plate, totally whole and untouched by such a fierce feminine. I don't even bother to stop and pick them up. Maybe, it is because I have already prepared myself to find nothing of value, nothing to connect me with the past, nothing to help me build for the future.

I pause, now and then, to steady myself and to sip some more water to calm the searing heat that wraps around my body. I notice an orange scissors peaking out through a pile of bricks. It is surrounded by broken glass. With gloved hand, I pick it up. Maybe, it is the pair of scissors that used to be in my office. It has begun to rust. I put it aside anyway. Maybe, it might be useful some day, I say to myself.

As I move on, I notice a picture cradled under some bricks. I pick it up. Immediately, I recognize it. It is a family picture taken in England in 1984 at my niece's wedding. It used to be in a frame and stood on top of the entertainment center in my bedroom. Now, some of the picture, sans the frame, is blotched and scarred, just like me. Maybe, it will remind me of happier times. So, I put it aside.

As I make my way, I discover a set of keys. It couldn't be but, then again, it could. They are the keys to my car. I know where I left them when I went on vacation and obviously, they have been moved by some cruel fate since then. I just throw them aside. I don't know why I would bother to keep them. Maybe, I am feeling a bit sad and nostalgic. But, then again, I need a reality check. The keys are memorable but not very practical now. Why? I don't have any car. They are simply the keys to a memory, to a past that emptied us of almost everything.

I continue on. I have no choice. I make mental notes of where things were. It is all past tense now, isn't it? That was an extra bedroom. The bathtub is still there. It is filled with broken tile, mangled fixtures and salt from a once pristine beach. Maybe, I might find something under all that? I am not too excited so I move on. There is the corridor, at least its outline. What is that blocking the back door? It seems to be suspended in mid air. It seems to be wedged in the doorway and just hanging on by a thread. I sure hope I hang on by more than a thread; otherwise, I am doomed to despair. It seems to be our refrigerator. I make a mental note. I need to find someone to help take it down as it may fall on some curious treasure hunter.

There is the outline of my bedroom. Against the outer wall, I remember a bookcase stood there. It was filled with magazines I had subscribed to over the years. It also housed the photo album of my ordination to the priesthood some thirty-three years ago. It was in black and white. But the situation I am facing now is not simply black or white; it is filled with the hue of complexity.

There on the wall, over my bed, hung the class picture of my ordination. The wall isn't even there now. Of course, the bed, where I rested my weary bones, probably is resting in the depths of the Gulf of Mexico.

What about my favorite recliner chair that sat, with open arms, in my bedroom? It was a going away gift from my former parish in Hattiesburg and I treasured it. I notice a piece of blue corduroy type furniture wedged in the corridor. Yes, it is a piece of that recliner. I think of the many nights I sat there to read or watch TV and eventually fell asleep in its arms. Now, its arms are broken; its back support is missing and its foot rest got tired and was wrenched away.

Then I notice a piece of rug crumbled up like a piece of paper guarding the corridor. I think it is blue but I am not sure. Peaking out from under part of it, I see something that looks familiar. Could it be part of my computer? How could it get washed all the way back here from my office? Maybe, I am in luck. Maybe, I will be able to salvage the hard drive and retrieve all the programs and information I had on it. Of course, I did have all my files backed up but they were probably backed up into oblivion in someone else's backyard miles away. I rescue the computer tower. It is battered and beaten. Its face is disfigured. I'm not sure it is really mine but it does look like it. I pull it out and place it in a plastic garbage bag. After all, it might be contaminated. I still hope for a miracle.

I notice pieces of clothing wrapped around some of the structure and nearby trees. I am not sure of their color but I am willing to claim them as my own. I am not even going to try and rescue them or try and bring their dead, colorless, odor-infected bodies back to life. I just move on.

Then, I notice a simple letter opener in the middle of a pile of bricks near the back door. I retrieve it and recognize it immediately as the one I used to use to open letters in my office at the other end of the building. It looks to be in good shape. I think I will keep this one. As I retrieve it, I remember who presented me with that letter opener. He was a parishioner in a former parish and was now living in Texas. I treasured this letter opener, not only because of Tim, who gave it to me, but also because its handle was in the form of a Celtic High Cross. It reminded me of my roots. Now, I wondered how much those Celtic roots and my Celtic spirituality would be challenged to support me in the long road to recovery of self, others and the community I served.

By now, hunger has surfaced. I sit down again in the shade of the still standing carport; open another bottle of water and take the two ham sandwiches I had packed earlier in the morning and begin to have lunch. Traffic moves up and down the street outside. I don't even bother to glance. After all, I am partially hidden from their view. I am also hidden in my own thoughts, fears and questions.

I decide to be brave again and take another stroll around the property. I am doing it, not to discover anything or to plan for anything. I am depressed enough; I don't need any more ammunition to exacerbate it. Maybe, I just want to do it to pass the time until Mary Ann arrives to take me away from this hell. My mind has had enough for today. It cannot absorb any more. I need to leave the rest of the torture to some other day. And I would like that torture to be spaced out over several days and months so I can still function.

Soon, curfew time arrives and I need to leave my shattered abode. Mary Ann arrives. She has been at her own home trying to salvage some items and memories that she treasures. She says, "There is only so much you can take every day." I agree. I have taken enough my first day.

We ride down the tree-strewn streets to where her family lived. We notice and we pass on to other areas. As we ride along North Beach, it resembles a war zone. There are no houses. Lots which once showcased elegant homes now support the embers of a cruel Katrina. Personal belonging, clothes in particular, dangle from naked tree stumps. May Ann points out where various people lived along the way. Now, their homes are cut down by a cruel hurricane. In their place, mangled trees and timber reflected the mangled lives of people who once had happy memories here. I am struck by the absence of people here. The city resembles a ghost town. Where generations of homes once stood along the beach, now a ravaged forest of trees, concrete, timber and mud sits.

As the evening twilight begins to embrace us, we turn toward the highway. The sights and sounds infiltrate our being. The stench of the stagnant, infected waters along the highway, fills our nostrils with revulsion. This is hell on earth and we have no choice but to embrace it. We are too tired to absorb it all. It will have to wait. How long will it take? What price will it exert? Do we have the stamina and resources to do it, whatever that "it" may be? Do I have the courage to face this hell and see it tamed, no matter how long it will take? Do I have the strength of character to be a beacon of hope in what initially is a hopeless situation? Is my faith strong enough to help rebuild my own life, the lives of my parishioners and the community? These thoughts and questions will have to wait for another day. My mind, body and heart cannot absorb any more today. These awkward thoughts and questions remain. Tomorrow is another day. Maybe, I will have more strength, and courage to carry this cross a little further.

3

Give Me a Call

It is Thursday morning and I am ready to do battle with the aftermath of Hurricane Katrina again. I survived yesterday, my first encounter with her calling card. Today, like a boxer, I have no choice but to answer another opening bell. I have to come our fighting. Will I have enough experience to throw a few punches today that might stun her? Do I have the fortitude to outclass her? Do I have the stamina to go toe to toe and punch to punch with her track record? Only time will tell.

First I need some boxing gloves as ammunition. I need a cell phone to connect me with the world as I call out over the airways for help and guidance.

I have never bothered with a cell phone before. I didn't wish to be tied down, to be "on call" all the time. I needed my own space without any airwave strings attached and I got it. Now, it is going to be different.

I stand in line at the only cell phone store in operation some twenty miles away. When I get there, a line of people meanders outside the store. We are all here for the same purpose. A security guard is on hand to make sure everyone behaves. I sign in and take a number and wait for the next available service representative to serve me. It reminds me of some calls I had made to computer technical support companies in order to receive help with a computer software program. While I am waiting, I browse through a sample of the various styles of phones and options that are available. I learn some new jargon; notice some "bells and whistles" extras being offered. I am just looking for something practical and functional.

Finally, my name is called. I decide on the phone style and options. Then I am asked, "Is there any particular phone number you are interested in?" I tell the service person that I need a phone number that is simple and easy for me and others to remember. He agrees and facilitates my request. My life is complicated enough without including more mystery and extra levels of sophistication.

Now, I have a phone. But there is a problem. Who can I call? I don't have anyone's phone number. Anyone who wishes to call me, cannot because they don't know my phone number. Yet, this cell phone will become my link with the wider world and hopefully, will generate a network of support, good will, guidance and help in the recovery process.

I journey back to Bay St. Louis again to continue the grieving process. Along the highway, things have not changed since yesterday. The same cars dot the highway. Some have run out of gas. Others have become victims of Katrina. As I get closer to the city, signs beckon us to slow down as a checkpoint comes into view. Military police man the roadway with their ever-ready M-16 rifles. They glance at each vehicle as it slowly passes their checkpoint.

Yesterday, I found my car keys. Today, I have no choice but to try and find it. I know the search will lead me to it. What will happen then, I am not sure. As I roam the neighborhood, I notice a group of thrashed cars a quarter miles away, just outside a cemetery. How ironic, I think to myself. I find mine—my 1998 Toyota Camry. It is crushed in like a crushed Coke can. It looks like a V-car. Its windshield broken into millions of pieces. I try to open the driver's side door. Eventually, it cooperates. I am not prepared for the odor that meets me. My faithful short umbrella sits in the side pocket. I rescue it. It is caked in mud. I check the glove compartment and am met with gushing water. I close it quickly and let it have its buried contents. I try and open the trunk. It will not budge. Inside, it holds my golf clubs captive. I give up. I summon up the courage to take some pictures of the car. I glance at the umbrella I had just retrieved and I hurdle it against the windshield. I turn around and leave, never to return.

Some parishioners come by the church to see for themselves. They try to be brave, indicating, "We will support you and we will be there for you." We all try to be brave but do we have the energy, resources and stamina to slay this dragoness?

Charles and his family stop by the church. He sees me and gives me a big hug. "It's great to see you. Glad you are here and safe." I ask him how he did through the hurricane. He has stayed with his son in Baton Rouge, some 200 miles away. Today, he returns for the first time to see his piece of heaven totally destroyed and replaced with a mountain of rubble. He had rebuilt after Hurricane Camille in 1969 and said he will try and do the same now. While we are talking, Vice President Chaney's helicopter buzzes overhear as it is being shielded by an array of other helicopters. No one bothers to even look up, realizing that the Vice President is really isolated from the plight of the people in the ghost town below.

As Charles and his family leave, I try to imagine what he is going through. Two years earlier, he took charge of the project to restore the church clock that is now mutilated; the chimes that called out the time was now silenced and the refurbished pipe organ that now has received a cancer death sentence from Katrina's wind and salt water.

As I sit in the debris of what used to be home, something crossed my mind. Where is my bike? I wonder. This hybrid bike with its twenty-seven gears was my early morning companion on the bike trail along the beach. It was a birthday gift from a good friend. Every morning at 4 a.m., she would coax me out of bed and onto her saddle for a ten mile morning ride. She opened my world to the early morning sights and sounds of a nature that gradually awakened from its slumber. She also reminded me of the need to be respectful and gentle with my body. She also afforded me an opportunity to pray a peddling prayer on the road to another day.

I look out at the beach road now. It is filled with sand and chunks of asphalt. When, if ever, will I journey down this road? Obviously, my bike has disappeared. I realize that, even if I could ride my bike down that road today, it would be like riding through a minefield as one would also have to dodge the hundreds of nails that would await the unsuspecting biker.

I catch myself regressing. I remind myself that nostalgia may provide a temporary diversion from the agony of Katrina but, deep down, I know it will not provide any support or direction for the future. I know I will have to dig deeper to find an answer that will carry me through this desolation into hope.

Two more ham sandwiches and a bottle of water become my lunch. I sit on that same chair as yesterday, easing the hunger pains but more conscious of the deeper pains that no ham sandwich can satisfy. As I eat, I look around and wonder if there might be anything else in the debris that could be salvageable. Maybe, I say it to myself just to give me some hope, something to hold on to; but, deep down, I know, it is just an escape thought.

I notice a small safe perched on the clean slab. It belongs to the rectory. I know it had been relegated to playing second fiddle to a newer, bigger and stronger safe. Where is that newer, bigger and stronger safe now? Like Jonah, it is probably swallowed up in the belly of the Gulf. It is amazing that a castaway safe survives while a more modern one disappears! Maybe, there is a message there for me. Still, I don't feel like philosophizing. I don't have the energy or desire.

On the way to my temporary abode, the military helicopters continue to hover overhead; the highway is awash with sirens from police cars from neighboring states. Some are on their way home, while others are making their initial visit to our ravaged city. Dozens of orange colored tree surgeon trucks form their own convey as they head home to various staging areas after a long and rewarding work day.

Two days in this hell, has given me a glimpse of the monumental task we all face in trying to rebuild our lives and community. There is frustration at the lack of presence and response of government agencies. Their staging areas are inadequate; their food distribution insignificant. People, in their anger, hurt, and frustration have turned to volunteers and churches from other states to offer them help. Grassroots groups have sprung up, free of governmental red tape and have come through for the people in their time of crisis. People have accepted the fact that they cannot wait for governmental agencies to reach or help them. Instead, they have summoned their inner strengths and begun to troubleshoot and do for themselves. Seeing that the major phone network is still down or working on a very limited and sporadic way, cell phones have become the new saviors of the people as they try to connect with each other and work together. For myself, there is the frustration of trying to establish a base in my parish. I cannot wait for a governmental agency to get me a trailer for such a base; I have to continue to make my own contacts and try and do it through the goodness and generosity of the people I know and am put in contact with. As I am faced with the anger, hurt, grief, and crushed lives of the people; I am overwhelmed by the goodness, generosity, empathy and courage of the ordinary person. Their comments are full of faith, and hope. Their comments epitomize their unquenchable spirit: "We will be back." "You can count on us." "Whatever it takes, we will do it." "If we can help, don't hesitate to call us. We will be there for you." Such hope, determined spirit and faith gives me inspiration and a faith in the goodness of people.

I know I will rest easier tonight, knowing that there are other shoulders ready to steer this ship of recovery through the turbulent waters of rebuilding and restoration.

4

The Suitcase Priest

I wake up Friday morning with an idea. Any idea, if it brings a touch of hope or a sprinkling of laughter to someone's life, is worth accommodating. I remember the old saying that says there is a fine line between tears and laughter. I know I will cross that fine line in both directions thousands of times over the next few months.

I laminate, with the help of Mary Ann's computer, a sign that reads, "Fr. Tracey—the Suitcase Priest." I include at the bottom my cell phone number. I also find a piece of plywood and spray paint—"Mass: Sunday @ 10 a.m."

Before I journey from Gulfport west to Bay St. Louis to begin another day sitting in the midst of the ashes of Katrina; I am visited with a very special person and prize. Eileen, a dear and long-term family friend, now living in Orlando, Florida, drives in with an unexpected gift. She brings me a tan colored 2004 Ford Tahoe SUV. A dealership in Hattiesburg, Mississippi has loaned it to me until I am able to purchase another car for myself. I am indebted to them for their generosity and thoughtfulness.

I climb into the SUV, armed with my signs and head toward Bay St. Louis. I feel elevated sitting in the driver's seat. I only wish my thoughts and future direction felt so elevated. Maybe, some day, they will.

I find a hammer and some rusty nails amid the debris and nail the signs to one of the electricity poles that is still standing nearby. I remember Marshall McLuhan's motto,—"The medium is the message." Yes, I have a message to impart and I have no choice but to be creative in getting that message out.

Of course, it helps to have a sense of humor which can get one through lots of tragedies. I know I will need lots of it in the days and months ahead.

I notice, as people drive slowly down the street, they pause and chuckle at my sign. I'm glad they get the message as well as see the humor in it. Some, armed with digital cameras, snap away at the sign. Maybe, the message will grace the hearts and homes of people. Hopefully, it may move them to respond.

Some visitors see a vehicle and realize that there is some life among the dormant embers. They stop and chat. Sooner or later, they ask the same question: "Where were you for the hurricane?" I indicate that I was in Ireland on vacation. "You must have been very lucky you were not here," they retort. "Yes," I reply. "This must be an awful mess you came back to?" they ask. I agree, without going into any more detail. I keep my own uncertainty sealed deep inside, at least for now.

I still need some quiet so I disappear into the troubled buildings with their wet, mud infected, contaminated floors. I pick my way through smashed ceiling tiles, piles of crushed glass and brick; mangled furniture and waterlogged TV's. I have to be careful on the slick floor as I don't want to slide into oblivion. Armed with my digital camera, I collect some more evidence. Maybe, I want to document "before and after." I am not sure but I feel the urge to capture the extent and volume of the destruction.

I make my way through desecrated classrooms, corridors incapacitated by huge lockers strewn on the ground as they vomit their belongings. There is no one to distract me or engage me in conversation. I don't have to explain or answer any questions. I like my space now and I need it. There will be other times I will need to be "available" to people, but now, I need to be available for myself.

Soon, it is time to bid farewell to the mess and head east to my temporary home in Gulfport. As I do, I bring with me another bucketful of the day's experience. It overflows with raw feelings, unanswered questions, and an overwhelming sense of loss. I don't even bother to turn on the radio. Right now, the only world that matters is the world within me. I am isolated from the traffic that rides the road with me. I am in my own mobile world. I am immune to the many exits I am to pass as I try to distance myself from the devastation, even momentarily.

Later this evening, I hear the sounds of heavy vehicles outside the business. Like a group of children awaiting Santa, we go outside to discover who this modern day Santa might be. A convoy of pickup trucks and an 18-wheeler truck supporting a large metal container ride into the parking lot with its crushed stone. There is a sense of anticipation for crushed spirits. A group of gentlemen alight from the convoy. Some look familiar. Mary Ann's brothers, Chuck, Kenny and Steve, as well as some of their friends arrive bringing glad tidings of great joy.

After hugs and brief introductions, it is time to unload. We form a human chain to unload suitcases of new clothes; a washer and dryer; mattresses; bed linens and, yes, food—Texas style. I stand aside and watch the ritual and happy faces. The Grinch who stole Christmas is now replaced by a group of Easter Bunnies from Texas.

The gift bearers hand out their gifts. Chuck hands me a bag of toiletries—a very timely and necessary part of a non-existent grooming wardrobe. Some time later, he hands me a red sports duffle bag. I lay it aside to open in a private moment later. I continue to watch as the container on the 18-wheeler is unloaded. Minutes later, Chuck gives me a large black garment bag. It is heavy. Like the others, I put it aside. Later I will unravel its contents. Some time later, a see a red Schwinn bike appear from the back of the container. He wheels it toward me, Chuck simply says, "I know you lost your bike. This is for you." I could feel tears well up as I tried to compose myself and be strong.

Some time later, we sit down to a lasagna dinner, prepared by Mary Ann. I listen in on the network of conversations which fills the air as the aroma of goodness, caring and family togetherness permeated the atmosphere.

Later, I steal some private moments to uncover the gifts I received. There, in the duffle bag, I discover an array of T-shirts, a collection of socks, pairs of sneakers and jeans. The black garment bag reveals a collection of "official" clothes—black suits, black pants. Now, I am truly in the black, I think to myself.

As I try to usher myself to sleep, I feel overwhelmed by the generosity of our visitors from Texas. They have come, not only bearing gifts, but also willing to do some cleaning out and, possibly retrieving some family heirlooms from their boyhood homes. I reflect on how, during the past week, Chuck has been calling his sister nightly, asking about my size. Reluctantly, I provided such information. Now, the results are gifts beyond compare. The ache in my heart is less painful now. I am truly grateful and blessed to have such wonderful friends. Amid tears of joy and a generous supply of hope that has been renewed, I know I will survive as I fall into the arms of sleep.

Saturday morning arrives early as all are ready to leave and help with the clean-up. By 8 a.m., everyone is on their way to Bay St. Louis. I drive along on my own in my temporary vehicle. The sun is shining. The day promises to be hot and we will be open to see what is ahead.

I stop at one of the local funeral homes. The other one has been destroyed. I think ahead. I want to leave my new cell phone number with them so they can get in touch with me to arrange funerals in the coming days and weeks. I find some of the funeral home personnel in a daze, trying to cope with their thrashed but manageable facility. Given their position in the community, they receive priority and have their phone services restored almost immediately. I ramble around the property once again, in a daze, amid my own thoughts and feelings, walking aimlessly amid the rubble. People constantly drive up and down the road and beachfront. Slowly they pause now and then to take a picture and then move on. One wonders if they are just sightseers or local people wanting to capture a disaster as it continues to unfold. Who cares! We are all in our own thoughts and cocoons, journeying through our own inner turmoil that hopefully, one day, may lead to healing and wholeness.

I need to see my totaled car once again to see if there is anything there that can be salvaged. I know I had decided not to return to it, but something compels me to return now. I look in the glove compartment for the car's license but am met with more slime and I withdraw my hand immediately. My insurance company will have to trust that I am—now was—the legitimate owner of the car.

I decide to head off to State Farm claim's office to see what kind of compensation I will receive for my wrecked car. Two rows of seats greet me; one is for just automobile and the other for home owner's insurance claims. Soon, I am called in and sit down to have my claim processed. Luckily, I have my insurance card in my wallet. I don't have to worry about the title of the car. Magically, the lady goes on line and connects with Jackson and finds it. Twenty minutes later, I leave with a check for over 9,000 dollars as well as a sinking feeling that I now have to turn around and buy another car. I had hoped that my Toyota Camry would live happily ever afterwards, giving me years of dedicated service and reliability but a kleptomaniac called "Katrina," stole part of my heart away. I am a bit philosophical as I realize that one chapter ends and another begins. I have brought closure to an era as I wonder who and what will help me write the next chapter.

Some people drop by and let me know that Jim, the maintenance man, is in the area and looking for me. He shares his story of rescue from the rafters of the Community Center and tells of some of the things he has found amid the rubble. He leaves to walk with some Seabees to point out some clean up work they could do, I stay there in my own thoughts.

I watch people stop and go into our church. They wonder at how sturdy it had been in spite of the hurricane. Minutes later, they exit, bringing with them a deeper appreciation for the sacred and how it stands as a testament to power of the Almighty.

Some people stop by and ask when school with restart. I tell them and it gives them a marker in order to plan the future, especially the future of their children and their welfare.

Others drop by and I receive a hug and an acknowledgement of happy they are to see me. It reminds me of my Father figure status in the community and how people look to me for guidance, direction and hope. I hope I will not disappoint them in the weeks and months ahead.

A returned phone call leads to scheduling a funeral at our sister parish because of the damage to our church. It is ironic that I have the same birthday as Pansy. It should be an interesting experience on Wednesday.

Soon, it is time for lunch. I get my small ice chest with its three turkey sandwiches and bottles of water and head into what used to be the carport. As I find a clean chair to sit down on and stare into space, my mind dwells on the catastrophe and its future implications. Amid the bricks, smashed glass, twisted metal, my own thoughts bring me within to my own twisted feelings, questions and struggles. Almost cut off from the gaze of the sightseers who pass on nearby Union Street, I wonder about their thoughts as they video and take digital shots of the destruction that envelops all of us. I wonder about their situation: are they just sightseers or are they too victims of Hurricane Katrina?

Soon, it is time to ramble off again to try and discover. I wonder what I can discover at this stage. I just ramble aimlessly around through the broken glass, bricks, timber, crushed dreams and crushed memories. There is a faint hope that I might find something to connect me to the pre-Hurricane Katrina times. Maybe it is just wishful thinking but I keep looking and hoping for something to connect with my past. The journey continues.

As the day progresses, so do the distractions. Photographers and journalists want my time and comments. They are interested in sound bites and I am not really interested in sounding off. They have a job to do, yet, somehow, they too are caught up in the emotion of the experience. One photographer, Susan who freelances with "The New York Times" walks aimlessly around the property, survey the damage, trying to anticipate the best location for a picture and stopping people along the way to get some comments.

As I walk along the beach front, she approaches me and asks some questions. When she finds out I am the pastor, an air of realism hits her. She simply but somehow sincerely says, "I am so sorry." In the quiet awkwardness that follows, she finally asks if it is okay to take my picture. I consent. We chat about where she is from, etc and I ask if she would be willing to send me some of the pictures. She says she will. She also says that she will be at Mass tomorrow morning and if it is okay for her to take some pictures there also. I consent. She asks if I would like a cold drink. She goes to her Volkswagen beetle car and brings me a lukewarm bottle of Gatorade. I accept her gracious offer and cool myself off from the unbearable sun.

Other reporters come—one from Catholic Charities, based in Florida. They want to set up a distribution center. I let them know some of the logistics and situations I am facing. They seem to understand and yet, I want to avail of their offer and services. They also bring their own photographer. I take the person's name and number and promise to call him when I get things more organized.

Chuck and his group visiting from Houston arrive to survey the damage to the church, rectory and schools. They ask if they can do anything. I tell them, not really. They have been busy all day trying to clean up their family members homes in the area. They notice the large stone cross that has been dethroned in front of the church. Immediately they erect it again and our New York Times photographer rushes in to take the picture. The group walks through the rectory and energetically tries to see if there is anything discoverable beneath a roll of soggy carpet that guards the corridor. They just discover a pile of crushed bricks and leave disappointed. I know they are trying to give me some hope but realism overcomes their anticipated wish.

Some time later, we decide to call it a day and head to Gulfport for the night. Texan steaks and baked potatoes are on the menu, courtesy of the group from Houston. They too arrive back and share some experiences as well as a hearty meal. They talk about their first impressions of the destruction they have witnessed. They share some of the items they have salvaged from the homes of their families. They try to give a glimmer of hope to those who have to lie in their beds of rubble.

Some time later, I excuse myself; find my way to my air mattress and try and let go of another day. My body wants to sleep but my mind will not cooperate. Eventually, they both meet by mutual consent and I rest in an uneasy peace.

5

Get Me to the Church

It's Sunday Morning. No! It may be "Sunday Morning" on CBS but it is going to be a different Sunday morning here on the Mississippi Gulf Coast. I know I will not have the honor or opportunity to watch the CBS program this morning. I have more important things to do and view. After all, I have my own Sunday morning experience that awaits me.

The Houston group wants to leave around 7:30 a.m. for their long trip back to Houston. All are up and ready to leave after a breakfast of coffee and cinnamon rolls. A series of hugs and they are ready to leave. We all gather outside the business to watch them tune up their engines for an exit. As their trucks turn around in the parking lot and turn toward the west, they give a final tug on the 18-wheeler's horn. We wave and they disappear down the road with more waves and goodbyes. It was a wonderful experience having them as they brought with them, not only food, gifts, clothing and necessities but also a love and dedication as well as a willingness to help.

Soon, it is time to head to Bay St. Louis again. I gather my supplies for Mass, wear my long blue pants and head off with my small ice cooler, complete with some water and a few sandwiches. On the journey there, my mind is flooded with thoughts of what to expect. This will be the first time I will meet my parishioners since the hurricane in a more formal setting at Mass. I wonder who will be there; what should I say that might give them hope and be a rallying cry. As I drive along Interstate 10, on my way there, my emotions begin to kick in and I try to fight back the tears and take hold of myself. It becomes obvious to me that I really love these people who are my extended family. I realize I have invested the past five years of my life with them. I remember celebrating beginnings and endings with them. I shared in their joys and sorrows; their celebrations and family meals. We have laughed and we have cried. Now, hopefully, we will be tested and hopefully, not found wanting but, instead, continue to recover our pride, dignity and even our stretched faith.

Before long, I am there, still wondering who will attend. We find two metal folding chairs and place a mangled piece of plywood on them to form an altar. We grace it with a white but soiled sheet. We hope the Lord understands. After all, centuries earlier, Mass was celebrated on the tombs of martyrs in the Catacombs. Now, we are about to celebrate it on a makeshift altar with people who are involved in trying to restore their own makeshift lives.

As I set up for Mass, with the help of Ethel, our sacristan and Ed. our music director, I try to gather my thought in anticipation of what is to come. People gradually filter around. The chairs are placed around the perimeter of the main entry way doors to the church. The altar is set up on the top step between the great columns that define its character. I wonder if Hurricane Katrina will continue to define my character. I have a sense it will.

I see some people working in our nearby property at the Community Center. I head off there to see who is doing it, but deep down, I am trying to find a distraction from what I know I will have to face during Mass. I notice Kevin. He is clearing off the tons of sand that cover our roadway and parking area. He wants people to negotiate their way to church and find some parking area. We chat as he shuts off his bulldozer and we head toward where Mass will be celebrated.

People begin to gather for our 10 a.m. Mass. Most, when they see me, came forward for a hug and a reminder that it is good to see me. We share some pleasantries and a reminder that, together, we will rebuild.

Kathleen, our Pastoral Associate, reminds me that "this is going to be a difficult Mass; that there is going to be a lot of emotion involved." I agree with her and tell her that it is going to be tough and emotional for me also.

We gather among the chunks of asphalt, naked trees, and sand filled grasses to offer to God our questions, our helplessness, our fears and our faith and trust that he will be with us for the long journey of rebuilding our hearts, homes, businesses and community.

The readings are over and it is time for the homily. I have thought a lot about what I might say at this time. I know I need to be empathetic; I know that most of these 250 people lost many possessions and some, I know, lost family. They are looking to me to give them hope and reassurance. They are looking for leadership and I hope I am up to the challenge.

I begin my homily with three words: "We are alive." I notice heads nodding in agreement. The rest of the homily includes some reflections and thoughts about working together to build our lives, our parish and our community. My thoughts and comments are often interrupted by applause and nodding of heads. Now, I know that people are waiting to hear the things I am saying. At the end of my homily, as I planned, I ask if some people wish to share their story of the hurricane and its impact on themselves and their family. Gradually people rise, come to the front and share their story. Often they fight back the tears but the dam begins to burst and the tears flow freely. As I look out into the eyes of the sun-scorched congregation, I can see and hear the sniffles. I try to fight back my own and am fighting a losing battle. I know I have to be strong for these people but I am also human. Every person who shares their story reminds us of how blessed we are. I am proud of these people; honored to be part of their lives, especially at this painful time in their lives.

Two and a half hours later, we end the Mass. Before doing so, I updated the people about what is happening through my eyes that might be of interest to them; the various groups willing to help and adopt the parish; the need for some sort of warehouse for distribution and of course, my need for a base at the church which means that we need a trailer or something of that nature to let people know I am back and available for them in their great loss and sorrow.

I remind them of the irony of the day. It is September 11. We remember another tragedy that visited our shores four years earlier.

Following Mass, people stay around and visit with each other. There is a show of solidarity and support. Some gather around me, sharing offers of various kinds—places to stay, food, and various other contacts. George offers a camper/trailer and I accept the offer. Now, I may be able to have a more permanent presence among the rubble to help people sort through the rubble and debris in their own lives. Later that afternoon, he drives into the parking area by the rectory and positions the travel trailer. I am blessed with a generator for power. It is another step in getting things organized and a little stability in the situation we face. Now, I have a base and a place to operate from. Again my Irish sense of humor and ability helps me see the possibility in the meanest of circumstances. I decide to make a sign and put it on the front of the camper. It reads, "Fr. Tracey's Condo." It brings a smile to the people who come by. I know that anything that gives us a chuckle and a momentary reprieve from the disaster is worth trying. After all, I am supposed to be in the business of sharing "good news."

Some families invite me for lunch. I tell them that I will have to wait and see how things develop. They give me their address. Finally, around 1:30 p.m., I find some quiet time and am able to go and enjoy a meal on paper plates—a roast, mashed potatoes, corn and even dessert. It is a welcome reprieve from ham or turkey sandwiches and bottled water.

Later in the afternoon, another journey begins for an important person in our parish. Jo, our Parish Secretary arrives. She is immune to the people who are gathered a short distance away. She gets out of her rented car and stands in front of the devastated rectory. She has worked in this building for the past eight years. She knows every corner; every piece of furniture; every closet; every color throughout the building. She seems to stand there for a long time as if incredulous; hoping that what she was seeing was not real but was a mirage. Finally, we notice that she begins to move slowly, picking out her way through the building. She pauses along the way, as if she is trying to figure out the floor plan. This is her first time seeing the destruction of her workplace. We allow her to go through the destroyed rectory at her own pace. We do not want to infringe on her private thoughts and grief. She stands on the slab where once her office sat. Now, it is a roofless space without walls or windows or any of the items she used to add her own personal touch to the office.

We watch her as she leaves the rectory area and moves to the church. She spends a few moments inside and then proceeds to our Community Center. Finally, she is ready to meet us. We hug and I wait for some reaction or response on how she feels seeing her spiritual home and workplace in shambles. She is not able to talk about it. We respect her privacy and allow her the space and time to grieve her loss. Eventually, she tells us that she had gone by to see her home before she came to the rectory. Her house had eight feet of water in it because of the hurricane. She mentions that she was not able to go into the house. Instead she sat outside in her car for a few minutes and realized that she could not face the trauma so she turned away. She finally broke down and cried, releasing her emotions and fears. She didn't need to be strong for anyone. She just needed to be herself.

Some time later, an attorney, one of our musicians for our Sunday evening Mass, comes by and we stand outside the church. He is a convert to the Catholic faith from years earlier. He talks about what the church means to him and as he does, he breaks down and cries. He ends with, "But we will be back again and we will rebuild." Then he apologizes and walks away.

Later, toward evening, a firefighter from Boulder City NV, comes by with a U-Haul truck of supplies, including clothes, camping equipment, tents, food and water. We store it in the driveway for now, hoping that people will be able to avail of it later.

As evening dawns, a group of people working on cleanup in the area come by wondering about evening Mass. I tell them that I will say Mass for them in a few minutes. I don some soiled vestments and celebrate the Mass for about 20 people. After some last minute clean up and closure, I leave for the drive to Gulfport.

As I drive away, I recreate the day in slow motion in my head. I reflect on the group of people who gathered for Mass earlier. Many of them had heavy hearts. Some tried to shade themselves from the scorching sun with umbrellas they rescued from flood infested homes. Others tried to seek shelter under the limbs of now bare trees. Most of them were immune to the presence of TV cameras, reporters and photographers trying to get a sound bite or the perfect shot.

I decide to do some laundry—the first since I arrived back from vacation. I pour in a generous amount of washing power and set the dials. I wait to hear it engage and disappear. I wish it were as easy to launder my soiled, confused and messy thoughts and fears. I know it will take a different kind of detergent and many more cycles to eradicate the stain of Hurricane Katrina.

6

What Do We Do Now?

Another week begins. Where do we go from here? What is ahead? What hopes do we have? What surprises might attack us? Who will come to help us? We begin the week with realistic hopes and are open to be overwhelmed.

On my journey, I ponder and wonder how desperately I want to control things; make them happen my way, in my time frame. Yet, I realize how little control I have. There are so many loose ends because of the hurricane. Because I do not have that control, frustration sets in. No matter how I try to plan or manage things, they never seem to work out.

As I journeyed along, I listen to an interview with the novelist, P.D. James on National Public Radio. He talks about control and our need to be in control. We try and dissect our lives into small manageable pieces, so we can have a better chance of being in control of our lives. As I listen, I begin to understand that control is one of the major problems I am having as a result of Hurricane Katrina. I am discovering one of its valuable lessons. I begin to realize that it is irrational and even insane to think that I can be in control of anything. I know that, as I travel through the next few days and weeks, I will be humbled even more into accepting this reality.

My mind carries me in different directions. I think about the many A.A. persons I have helped work through the fourth and fifth steps of the program. They, too, thought they were in control; that they could control their drinking or drug use. I begin to realize that Hurricane Katrina has brought me to a "crunch time;" the humbling realization that I am no longer in control and if I accept that fact, then, maybe, I will be freer to see the big picture.

School teachers call to find out what is happening with our Elementary School. They are anxious to find out and make plans in spite of their own personal losses.

A group of Seabees drive in and want to help with the clean up in our school. We direct them to begin the clean-up in the school cafeteria. Some time later, I check on them and notice that they are creative in the ways they are cleaning out the mushy mud. I notice that they are using a six-foot table turned on its side and they are using the feet to push the mud out into the hot sun. It is a reminder of how ill-prepared we are to deal with such a catastrophe.

The pastor of the neighboring parish drops by. His church, school and parish offices, as well as his residence are totally destroyed. He seems desperate and wonders how he is going to cope with the situation. I offer him some advice and suggestions which seem to help.

In the middle of our conversation, Jerry from Wisconsin calls. He called last week and is looking for an update so he can begin to direct some volunteers in our direction. I share with him some of the major obstacles we are facing. He asks about communications. I inform him that it is almost non-existent. We chat about various possibilities to remedy the situation, including procuring a satellite phone system.

Later, some more Seabees arrive and want to help with the clean up. I ask them if it is possible for them to put tarp on the roof of our church in order to preserve the paintings on its ceiling in case it rains. They are not able to do it as they do not have the equipment needed for the job. I then ask them about the possibility of pumping out the basement of our church. The stagnant water is becoming a breeding ground for all kinds of germs and infections. They indicate that they are not able to get a pump to do the job. As they leave, they indicate that they will be back in the morning with some equipment. They forget to come. I think to myself, it is a "hurry up and wait" approach. The resources needed to begin the remedial work are non existent and I have to deal with the frustration that follows.

Later that afternoon, I decide to leave the luxury of the air conditioned camper and stroll around the church area to see who might be around and to be in my own thoughts. As I walk down the memorial walkway toward our miraculously untouched shrine to "Our Lady of the Woods," my cell phone rings. Even in the midst of such chaos and desolation, there is hope and even communication. My sister, Eileen, is calling from England. It is quite a surprise and we chat for thirty minutes. I update her with all that has happened since I came back from Ireland as well as the progress and the attitude of the people, along with the generosity of people from outside.

Some time later, I notice some parishioners walking toward the church. It is a welcome sign to see people come and find out how the church survived the hurricane. An elderly parishioner, Luke, and his family are there. He tells me about his ordeal through the hurricane and how he floated out an attic window that was smaller than his body frame. The water carried him onto the roof and eventually to safety. He felt a hand on both shoulders, carrying him to safety. In the week since the hurricane, he has been moved five times from one shelter to another. He is anxious for some stability and normality in his life and knows that it will be in short supply in the months ahead. He thanks the Lord for saving his life and still wonders why he was saved.

Yes, what do we do now? We have no choice but to trust that some doors will open; some phone calls will be answered; some gifted volunteers will arrive. These are my thoughts and questions as I begin another day in the recovery process.

Breakfast is simple—two cinnamon rolls and a cup of hot tea. I am ready for the thirty mile journey to Bay St. Louis again. The Interstate is busy with supply trucks making their way to some ravaged area—hopefully, some are going to mine. I pass a convoy of tree surgeons on their way to another site. Later, I expect to hear the whining of chainsaws in the air.

Shortly after arriving, I notice some Corps of Engineers personnel and ask them if they would be willing to put tarp on the roof of our church. Firstly, they suggest that we contact our insurance company if it is okay for them to do the job. Secondly, they indicate that they need to assess the situation first before they commit. Finally, the answer is negative. They are only putting blue tarps on private residence. We do not qualify. The old adage, "hurry up and wait," is still alive and well.

Hunger pains clamor for attention and I tame them with a dash of gumbo and chicken stew, courtesy of one of the feeding places. Later, it became affectionately known as "Brennan's on Bookter Street," deriving its name from the famous Brennan's restaurant in New Orleans.

Some fellow priests drop by and are spellbound by the extent of the destruction. They tour the area and remind me of the enormous task that lies ahead for me. I only know too well.

Later, Jerry calls me from Wisconsin. He has done some research on a satellite phone system. Companies are not willing to sell him one unless they can install it and it would be three to four months before they could do so. Another door closes. Maybe, a window might open in its place. We hope and pray.

Some minutes later, a window does in fact open. John, who is a manager for Home Depot in Atlanta, arrives with a supply of practical gifts for the parish that will aid our clean up. He is amazed at the volume and extent of the destruction. He is from All Saints parish in Dunwoody, Atlanta and he becomes a catalyst in the recovery process in our community. Maybe, there is a light at the end of the tunnel and it is not a train heading toward us. Maybe, a day which began with some deep inner rumblings and insights, can end with a more hope-filled future filled, now unknown, yet exciting possibilities.

Another morning dawns. It is 4 a.m. and I am awake. I dare not get up and disturb the rest of the people sleeping on the floor. I just lie there in my own thoughts and rehash in my mind what has happened so far. When I think of the progress that has been made, I get a good feeling; then I think of the obstacles I have faced in getting things done and it is easy to get discouraged. I think I have taken some steps forward. Still, I realize that I dare not continue to see life through the rear view mirror solely; otherwise, the future will come knocking on my door and I will not be able to hear it.

As I drive along Interstate 10 on my way to Bay St. Louis, I have my own thoughts, muddled as they are, but no time to be sorry for myself. People are depending on me for leadership and direction and I have to be strong for them too.

I drive down Highway 603 on my way to Bay St. Louis. I pass the stagnant waters that give off a horrific odor. Along the way, cars are still strewn along the highway, all waiting to be picked up by insurance companies. They are all totaled.

I notice an old woman walking by the side of the road. She is supported by a walking stick and is carrying a radio in her other hand. It is her lifeline to the outside world. As I pass by her, I remember that I have not read a newspaper, watched any TV since I arrived from Ireland. I have no desire to tune in any more noise than what rumbles inside me. My own thoughts and feelings are more important than some of the idle chatter that often permeates the airwaves.

It is time to apply a generous supply of suntan lotion, get my cell phone, my note pad and head into the unknown day.

As I ramble around amid the debris, I wonder what this day will bring. Will there be progress? Will there be surprises? I know I have my first funeral in a short time at a nearby church. That is going to be a painful experience for all involved but together, we will survive.

A burly gentleman shouts at me from across what used to be the parking lot. He calls my name. I introduce myself. He introduces himself as a firefighter from Long Island, New York. "I have come to help you," he said, "What do you want me to do?" We chat a little about our experiences of the New York area and I take him and introduce him to Jim, our Maintenance person. As he heads in that direction, the firefighter says, "I thought I saw it all in New York with 9/11 but this is much worse." I leave him in Jim's hands and head off to take care of other things.

As I continue to write my thoughts, there is a knock on the door of the camper. It is Mike, another angel in disguise. He is coordinating getting some tarp on the roof of the church so that our beautiful painted ceiling will not be ruined by rain. I update him on the roadblocks we have encountered. He tells me of the efforts he has made to get the army to do it but also has met roadblocks. He drops off the tarps and leaves his cell phone number. He informs me where he got the tarps which had to be big enough to cover the church's roof. His brother works for an outdoor advertising company and has procured some of their large, heavyweight plastic advertising signs. Most of the signs happen to be advertising for some liquor companies. Mike assures me that he will make sure the advertising part is hidden from an aerial view. Obviously, we do not wish to offer free advertising in our church. We both see the humor in it and it helps lighten the pressure load we bear.

Later, I receive a call from Nancy in Hattiesburg. She tells me that her son, Stephen, who works with networking at USM, has put the digital pictures I have taken and comments on the Web. She gives me the address as: http:\\hightide.st.usm.edu\katrina. Again, we discover another window on the world through which we can communicate with the world and allow people to journey with us in the recovery process.

A short while later, some troops arrive with wheelbarrows, shovels, gloves, water and backpacks. They are ready to sift through some of the debris piled up on our property near the school. I visit with them, find out they are from Nova Scotia mostly and they spring into action. They are organized and begin separating the thrash into piles—some that might be personal, some that is lumber, some that is equipment and some that can definitely be discarded. Chatting with them, I discover that they arrived in Pensacola, Florida a few days earlier by ship. They mention that it was their first experience on a naval vessel. The Commander informs me that he will be flying back instead of going by sea.

Shortly afterwards, it is time for my first funeral since the hurricane. It is being held at a nearby Catholic church because ours has been badly damaged. I change into a black pants and black clerical shirt for the occasion. As I do, I realize that this is the first time I have worn my official garb since returning from vacation. Following the funeral, we journey through streets and property, filled with destruction and decay and make our way into a soggy cemetery where the substitute hearse gets stuck. Both funeral home hearses got destroyed and they were using a vehicle with which they collect bodies. The experience brings home the irony of the situation.

Immediately on returning from the funeral, I change from my official garb to my hurricane attire. First, hunger pains need to be abated. There are three turkey sandwiches left over from 3 days ago and I munch on them amid phone calls.

Now, it is time to be generous again with the Coppertone and get ready to go our again in the midday sun. As I am about to head out, a fellow priest from a neighboring parish drops by. He cannot believe the destruction, shakes his head and says, "I wouldn't want to be in your shoes." I tell him we have to work with the burden that is placed on our shoulders. Of course, I wish it were different and didn't have to face what often seems an overwhelming situation. But, I remind myself that we cannot always choose the path laid out for us.

A parishioner drops by to see our church. She says that her home and the homes of most of her children have been destroyed. She mentions that the first question she asked her children after the hurricane was: "How is my church?" When she found out it was still standing, she was delighted. She left with her own memories. Then, I realize the power of a church's presence as it stands as a beacon of hope, even when it is being buffeted by hurricanes.

I still need a place to call "home." I need to sign up with FEMA (Federal Emergency Management Agency). I hear all kinds of stories of how difficult it is to sign up. People are met with busy signals and holding on the phone for hours. Some are resorting to staying up and calling at two or three o'clock in the morning. I am blessed to have a good, family friend, Eileen, troubleshoot the sign up for me and help me.

Some days later, Eileen calls me to inform me that FEMA does not know me; that I don't exist; that there is no such social security number. I wonder if I have become the Invisible Man. I realize that the Internal Revenue knows me and my social security number. I wonder why FEMA doesn't know it or wonder if there is a communication problem. Anyway, I remind Eileen to keep trying. She does.

Before I leave for the evening, I take one more stroll along what used to be the beach. Complete with my digital camera, I pick my way through the chunks of asphalt, broken up concrete, maze of electrical wires and sand. I snap a few pictures and meet two Baptist preachers from California. They are here to access damages and see how their communities and churches can help. I give them my name in the hopes that maybe something may happen.

As I drive home to Gulfport again, I realize this is not "home." I do not have a home right now. I go around with a cell phone and notepad that become my lifeline to the community and outside world.

The next morning, I am awake at 5 a.m. I just lie there and wonder what this day will bring. I wait for Mike and Mary Ann to get up and attend to their business. At 6 a.m., I decide to get up and shower and shave. It feels so good. Two pop-up tarts and a cup of tea allows me to take a breather before I hit the road.

I sit in the kitchen for a few moments with Mary Ann. We talk about, you guessed it, the hurricane. Is there any other topic of conversation? We discuss especially the psychological trauma on the children resuming school, whenever, and how that will impact them and if there will be counselors available.

When I arrive at the trailer I get the generator cranked up and the activity begins. The phone starts ringing; people have questions and there are no answers. People are asking questions that are long-term and it is hard to think beyond the immediate. Is this going to be another day at the office? I begin to realize that it is not just another day.

Our former bishop drops by. He is wearing a black pants, white shirt and his proverbial red suspenders. He talks about the destroyed rectory and how the pastor who build it in 1971—Msgr. Johnson—built it to withstand another hurricane. Obviously he never planned for one like Hurricane Katrina. Maybe it is a blessing that the former pastor died last year and is not around to see the death and destruction. The bishop visits the church also and has some questions about it being rebuilt. We share our hopes that it will.

Even in the midst of chaos and destruction, some things never change and that includes nature's call. I enter the portable toilet and am about to sit on its throne when my cell phone rings. I answer the caller's question and, as I am about to leave, the phone rings again. As it does, I remember a sign I once saw that said, "the phone will always ring when you are in the bathroom."

Soon it is time for lunch. I decide to check out the same place I went to two days ago for a hot meal. This time, they have barbequed chicken, string beans, red beans and rice. It is messy, but who cares. It is food and it will help for now. The Red Cross is in the area as I leave giving out vouchers and money. People are lined up for blocks in the blazing sun as they wait to cash in.

Afterwards, I decide to take a breather and head off with my camera around the schools. I walk by St. Stanislaus and snap some pictures of the piles of debris they have accumulated to be hauled away. I walk along the sand beach, maybe, hoping to see something I recognize. Maybe, I might even find our large safe on the water's edge. No luck.

As I walk along, I notice a familiar face—a man is walking down the street on his way to the beach. He has a bible in his hand. He is the gentleman who shows up in the area from time to time. He lives in a dark green Econo van. I'm sure he is thinking about how the complexion of the area has changed since he was here some months ago. I watch him and notice that he stops by the church, opens his Bible and begins to read. I hope he is praying for us and for all who worship in it.

As I am about to leave for the evening, a representative from State Farm Catastrophe Team comes by the area looking for some private property he has been asked to evaluate for insurance purposes. He says he is here to check it out structurally. He has a ladder in his pickup truck. I bring him to our neighbor's property and show him. I tell him that he doesn't need to use his ladder or worry about the structure. It is all gone. He says he will take a few pictures and leave. He has an easy task. I wish my task was as easy.

7

"How Are You Doing?"

The weekend arrives. Hopefully, it is an opportunity to meet some more of my parishioners and to continue rebuilding our lives, homes, church and community.

It is Friday morning and I awake at 4:30 a.m. I just lie there for a while on an air mattress, trying to sort out some unfinished thoughts and anticipate what might be ahead for just today. I know I need to keep looking at the big picture but one has only the energy to embrace one day at a time.

Breakfast is simple—a cup of hot tea and two pop-up tarts. I wish every decision was as simple. As I travel along Interstate 10 on my way to Bay St. Louis, I become very conscious of the tension in my neck and shoulders. I try to wiggle some of it out as I drive along but relief is momentarily. I know the cause of the tension and I know I have no choice but to live with it for the next few months, if not years. My only hope is that I can channel the tension into something creative and productive.

When I arrive in Bay St. Louis, I discover that BellSouth—our local phone company—has set up a phone bank in the parking lot of one of the destroyed shopping malls. Armed with my laptop, I drive to the phone bank and connect with my family in Ireland and England. Even though it is just 7 a.m. here; it is six hours later where my family lives. Once again, I am able to reconnect with them and give them a progress report amid helicopters buzzing overhead. The family ask me the obvious question, "How are you doing? Is there anything we can do for you?" Right now, my answer is non-committal and I just dispose of it quiet easily. Yet, deep down, I know I will have to try and struggle with an answer to that same question in the months ahead. Now, the tension in my neck and shoulders become a reference point toward a more honest answer.

Even though the question never leaves me, I try to answer it in my own mind by trying to work toward daily accomplishments, no matter how big or small. They become a barometer as to how the answer to the question will be framed.

I notice some Mississippi Power workers in the area. Maybe there is a chance that I might get some temporary power and not have to be lulled asleep by the sound of a noisy generator. They give me a sheet of paper with some instruction. Minutes later, a parishioner stops by. By coincidence, she also works for the same power company. I tell her about my desire and she indicates she will take care of it. I trust her and wait in hope. Maybe, now I can give a partial answer to the question, "How are you doing?" Obviously, I am doing better because I have more hope. I see the possibility of temporary power which would change the complexion of things dramatically. Later in the day, the same parishioner arrives to let me know that a temporary power pole will be installed tomorrow. The fog of doubt lifts a little and I live in hope.

Some time later, that glimmer of hope becomes tarnished when I am informed that our pipe organ needs to be removed for now. We had just spent $70,000 to renovate it. I am told that it will cost $20,000 to remove it and $60,000 to repair it. All the electronics are damaged. One would love to bury one's head in the sand and hope that all this is not happening, that it is a dream, but one has to face facts and reality; try and regroup and go on.

Before I leave some people from The Red Cross come by. They offer some drinks. I decline. They stop and chat. One of them is a Catholic from Wisconsin. She keeps asking me: "How are you doing?" I don't even have time to ask myself. I know I have to be strong for my people who will need a big shoulder to lean on and cry on during the next few months. I feel it is ironic that I have been asked the same question at the beginning of the day and now almost at the end of the day. I realize that I need to reflect some more on the question and honestly probe its depth for my own sanity and survival. I will do that later, of course.

On Saturday morning, as I gulp down some pancakes and wash them down with hot tea, I receive a phone call from my family friend, Eileen, who is calling from Orlando, Florida. She has been working on getting me registered with FEMA. She has a FEMA representative on another phone line and has gotten me "almost" registered with them, finally. Some more questions, I can answer and FINALLY, I get a claim number. Another milestone has been accomplished. Will I get anything from them? After all, I am displaced; have lost everything; will that matter? It should. They are supposed to send me some paperwork. I will have to wait and see what happens; be realistic and not get my hopes up. If I get some financial help, it will be great; if not, I can close that chapter and forget about them.

Finally, I head back to Bay St. Louis, my operations center for another day, hoping that progress will be made. Along the way, I pass 35 power company trucks on their way to power up some more homes. On the opposite side of the Interstate, there is a convoy of police cars heading east. They are coming off night duty. Suddenly, the traffic grinds to a complete halt just east of the Diamondhead exit. A highway patrol car blocks the three lane highway. People get out of their trucks and cars to find out what is happening. We are informed that the power company is putting a power cable across the highway and we have to wait until they complete the task. Ten minutes later, we are on our way.

When I arrive at the camper, my "condo," George is there and has fueled up the generator for another day. There is no sight of a roofing company for our church. Today, we are hoping that we can get a power pole installed so we can get a temporary power connection to our camper. We will have to wait and see.

I decide to go back to the BellSouth Phone bank where the company has set up about 20 phones for people to use. There are just a few people there so early in the morning so I grab a vacant line and call my family in Ireland. I talk to my brother, Tom, and update him on things; letting him know about our web site and some information he may be able to use.

When I finish the phone call, and return to my base of operations for the day. I apply a generous helping of suntan lotion and prepare to do battle with the sun. It is hot and humid already. Armed with my cell phone, notebook, pen, safari hat, I venture out.

I am surprised to meet Suzanne. She drove in from Alabama. She is a graduate of Our Lady Academy. Now married and with a family, she is visiting with her brother in Hattiesburg and comes into the area to see the destruction for the first time. She is also amazed. During the course of the conversation, she tells me that her husband, Terry, who is a helicopter pilot, is in Iraq for a year. She also tells me that they have extra gas in their truck and offers it to me. I gladly accept, especially for a generator and a SUV that is constantly hungry. Right now, I do not have the cash to keep filling it with gas.

Some parishioners drop by the church again for the first time. They share stories. The Smiths follow. Richard is too distraught to go into the church. The first floor of their home was gutted. There is sadness when they inform me that they will not be returning to the area. They have decided to relocate elsewhere.

At 12:30 p.m., there is progress. The electrician shows up with a power poll and begins putting it up. It is now 1 p.m. and the power poll is up. George has gone to get the temporary permit. The electrician says he will call his daughter-in-law with the Mississippi Power Company and have them connect the power.

Shortly afterwards, his daughter-in-law. drops by from Mississippi Power. She brings by the form to sign for the power company to hook up the power but the permit office is closed until Monday. She also comes bearing gifts—a chicken dinner with all kinds of trimmings that seem foreign to me. I eat the chicken and enjoy it and wash it down with a bottle of orange juice. It might seem strange to drink orange juice with a dinner but these are strange times and no one is standing on protocol.

Other parishioners visit the church for the first time and say, "I hope you are going to rebuild it." I simply have to say that I hope we can. In fact, we have no choice. We have to rebuild but first we need to know that the shell of the structure is structurally sound. We wait in hope but we plod on with perseverance.

David drops by to check on me and to bring some good news. We chat about our experiences and frustrations—he about insurance; I about trying to get simple things done. He mentions that CNN is going to be doing a documentary in the area; that Kathleen Koch, their reporter will be in the area on Tuesday. It is ironic that she is the one doing it as I know her and her family used to live in the Bay St. Louis area. I am looking forward to renewing acquaintances with her again.

It will soon be time for Saturday evening Mass at 5:30 p.m. and we will see who attends.

About 30 people attend for evening Mass. I update them on what has happened during the week. I also share with them some of the problems we have been having getting the roof of our church covered with tarp. We want to get the damaged roof of the church covered as soon as possible so that the beautiful paintings on the ceiling will not be destroyed. I share with them the need for a crane to get the materials onto the roof but that we have been unable to procure one. I ask if anyone can help, to please let me know.

As I head back to base, I receive a phone call from someone who attended evening Mass earlier and said they had tracked down a crane that might help us put the tarp on the church. Good news for a change. It will be available on Monday and will arrive from Jackson. I give him the contractor's cell phone number so they can coordinate it.

Sunday morning traffic is heavy, as we navigate our way to my "condo." I arrive around 8 a.m. and enjoy some quiet before people start gathering for Mass.

Soon people start arriving, with umbrellas to ward off the hot sun. They stop and chat with each other. No one is in a rush. There is a lot of hugging and kissing going on. A reporter comes by from Iowa and wants a piece of me. Some people from his area are down helping out. I give him a few sound bites and send him on his way.

Mass starts late but nobody cares. People are still visiting. The first reading from Isaiah is appropriate where it says that God's thoughts are very different and loftier than ours. I use it as a stepping stone to my thoughts in the homily. I mention that we are so busy, so organized with our palm pilots, our cell phones, our schedule makers, our appointments, our "to do" lists and deadlines and along comes a lady named Katrina and not only messes us up but destroys the crutches we have build to lean on and support us. I continue to remind people that we are alive; that we have each other and that we have hope and will come back.

Mass does not last as long as last week but that is okay. There were many more people there as well as people who were not there last week. Some updates were shared as well as announcements.

Following Mass, we have two baptisms, Walker Everette and Brynn Alyce. It is a historic moment as we try to do the baptisms in the shade of the entry way. I get an invitation to join the families for dinner afterward and accept. As I perform the baptisms, I notice the irony of the situation. We are in the middle of chaos, destruction and debris. It is also a death but we are celebrating a new beginning; a new hope, a new arrival. Maybe, there is reason to continue, reason to believe, reason to hope; reason to feel better.

I head back from the baptism celebrations and find the place is relatively quiet. As I begin to put my thoughts down, there is a knock on the door. I open the door and get a bear hug from a gentleman who is on his own. He has come to find out about re-registering his kids for school. We put him in touch with the principal. What is ironic about this gentleman and his family is that they were presumed missing and drowned. People feared they stayed in their home and were drowned. When he came in, he quoted Mark Twain:—the report of my immanent death has been greatly exaggerated.

I go out again. I notice some pictures and pick them up. Maybe someone, someday, will recognize them and claim them. Maybe they will help fill in some of the vacuums in people's lives. Maybe, there is a project there for someone—a photo recovery and restoration project. Do I really want to embrace such a project.

Part of me wants to help people reconnect with their memories, their past and their albums; another part of me, dismisses the idea because I am already in "overdrive" and don't need any more projects.

Later in the afternoon, I decide to go to the BellSouth phone bank and call my family. I talk with my sister, Eileen, in Coventry, England and update her. I then talk with my family in Ireland. My brother is not there but I talk with my sister-in-law, Mary and update them on progress, if any here. I also get a chance to talk with my other sister, Bernie who is visiting there.

During our conversation, my cell phone rings. Jerry is calling from Wisconsin. He reminds me that the first group of volunteers from his parish will be arriving here on Thursday. I know this will be just the beginning of a long and productive relationship. He asks if it would be okay for some high school student to come also. We indicate it would be a wonderful experience for a high school student to see it firsthand for themselves. It might also help them to appreciate the little things in life that we often take for granted.

As I drive down the Interstate, there is no phone call to answer which is a relief. I am in my own thoughts. Obviously, my own thoughts are complicated as I mull over that same question I continue to be asked by family, friend and stranger. "How are you doing?" Thoughts and feelings race through my mind at a pace faster than the 70 m.p.h. I am traveling. How can I capture them; corral them; make sense of them; put them in some kind of intelligible order? Is there really an answer to that question? Does the answer change from day to day depending on failures or accomplishments? I know I am facing no ordinary situation—thanks to Hurricane Katrina. Will she dictate the rest of my life; my attitude; my resolve; even my sanity? I anticipate having to troubleshoot my mind's overloaded circuitry. The only choice will be to try and put my thoughts on paper.

When I arrive in Gulfport, it is nice and quiet. There is no one around. Mike and Mary Ann have gone to Hattiesburg, bringing their daughter back to college. I do not know what to do with the quiet. I eat my leftover dinner from the baptism today and it tastes good. Then I decide to take a shower now rather than in the morning. The calm is refreshing but unusual. There is no one to tell about what happened today. I might as well enjoy the quiet while I have it, as there will be tough times ahead. But my mind will not cooperate. So, I power up my laptop and the traffic of ideas begins to flow onto the screen. As the thoughts begin to flow, I wonder if I will like what comes forth. Will I be able to decipher them? Will I find a pony in the middle of the manure?

As the words begin to flow, it is almost impossible to keep pace. My fingers cannot type fast enough to capture the hurricane of thoughts that want to break through. Yet, I have no choice but to continue to try.

Since Hurricane Katrina, I have been asked hundreds of times, "Is there anything I can do for you?" by parishioners, people on the phone, people who drop by, people who are complete strangers. I know the vast majority of my fellow priests have been asked the same question hundreds of times also.

It is heartening and humbling to know that people, genuinely, care enough to ask and just as sincerely want to help.

As priests, we all know why people ask this question, given the effects and trauma of Hurricane Katrina. But, what we find difficult to do is to answer it completely and honestly. We often dismiss the question or give a cursory answer. You may wonder why we do that and why your pastor does it when you ask him the same question. Well, the answer is deep and difficult. Let's try and understand it.

First of all, we need to think about expectations. Being a priest, like any profession or calling, brings with it a series of expectations. A priest is expected to or perceived to have all the answers, or, at least, most of them. There is also the perception and expectation that priests are strong, especially emotionally, and, so when he faces the havoc, trauma, destruction and overwhelming sense of helplessness following a catastrophe such as Katrina; he wants to make sure that people continue to see him as strong. He tries to live up to their expectations, but, deep down inside, he may be really confused, hurting, overwhelmed by the task of rebuilding. Still, people need to continue to ask their priest: "Is there anything I can do for you?"

Secondly, there is the trauma that people are experiencing following the hell of Hurricane Katrina. They have their own horror stories of destruction and despair; survival and stage fright. The priest has his own same stories, that are often multiplied hundreds of times but he doesn't want to burden you with them. In his estimation, your story is more important than his. Still, people need to continue to ask their priest, "Is there anything I can do for you?'

Thirdly, there is the question of pride. Priests don't want to be perceived as weak, as struggling, as confused, as overwhelmed especially in the enormous task many of them face in trying to rebuild their parish and faith community. They don't want to burden people with their own burdens. Still, people need to continue to ask their priest, "Is there anything I can do for you?"

Fourthly, there are the outside forces which impact the priest's rebuilding task. One such force is dealing with diocesan officials, insurance, contractors and the disharmony between the groups and the parish. The priest may wish to proceed with the rebuilding but his efforts are stymied by lack of direction, and the placing of obstacles in the way of recovery by people who do not have to work on ground zero day after day. The priest doesn't want to tell you about such frustrations because he might be branded as a maverick, not a cooperator. Still, people need to continue to ask their priest, "Is there anything I can do for you?"

So, in the light of Hurricane Katrina, people need to continue to ask that most basic question of their priest. In doing so, they will allow the priest to be a vessel of clay; a human being; a searcher for answers; a wellspring of good will; a builder of relationships and a discoverer of inner resources and strengths he may never know he had. Maybe, some day, when you are persistent, your priest will be free enough to answer honestly the question: 'Is there anything I can do for you?'"

8

Reconnecting

It is Monday morning, I wake up at 4 a.m. and search for my watch. My body wants to lie there on the air mattress. My mind wants to travel in all kinds of confusing ways. While I lie in bed, a troubling thought crosses my mind. My watch also says that today is Monday, September, 19th. It dawns on me that it is almost three weeks since Hurricane Katrina struck at that fateful time of 4:50 a.m. I ponder the enormity of the devastation as well as the enormity of the task ahead.

I celebrate that critical hour by having two pop-tarts and a cup of tea. I sit at the breakfast counter with Mary Ann. The conversation leads to family squabbles. Maybe, while we cannot solve them, at least, we can have a momentary diversion from more weighty matters, such as the impact of a hurricane on us personally and professionally.

As I travel to Bay St. Louis, there is a low lying haze surrounding us. Maybe it is symbolic of what people are feeling and going through right now.

On arrival, I discover my day will be a series of connections and reconnections. The first is how do you connect water—if there is any available—to the camper? Great minds discuss but the solution seems to evade them. Secondly, I miss some phone calls; get cut off and, when reconnected, cannot find the caller. Thirdly, we are still waiting for the building inspector to give us the okay to get the temporary power connected. He passes by once but didn't see the pole. It is getting late now and we might have another night without power. Fourthly, we spend some time trying to disconnect or dislodge a bus that is wedged between a building and a Cyprus tree. Fifthly, John, from Home Depot, drops by. He brings a truck load of practical supplies, including shovels, cleaning supplies, wheelbarrow, etc. Now, we can disconnect the debris around the place and reconnect it with the mountain that already stands by the roadside. Sixthly, I drive to the BellSouth phone bank and call my friends, Bill and Carolyn. I chat with Carolyn for a long time and update her on what has been happening. She is thrilled to hear from me as she was wondering what had happening to me. This is the first time we have chatted since the hurricane. I realize another milestone is reached in that good friends are reconnected and in touch again. Finally, on my return to the camper, following supper, I notice some streets lights on. This is another sign of progress. I am about to spend my first night in my adopted "Condo" trailer.

The next morning, I awake at 4 a.m.—the first night in the camper. The constant hum of the generator outside my window did not help. I just lay there and tried to put things in perspective. Obviously, I had a lot more questions than answers. Knowing that I could not go back to sleep, I finally got up at 6 a.m. I put on my clothes from yesterday and walked down to the portable toilets.

When I walk outside to go to the portable toilet, I notice a Florida Highway Patrol man just walking around. He stops and asks, "Are you Fr. Tracey?" I indicate "Yes." He mentions that he sent me an email. I let him know that we do not have access to Internet or email but that I would get it eventually. He then goes on to talk about his partner who was in the church crying. He tells me that his partner is not a believer and cannot make sense of what happened to the area. We talk some more about it and his partner finally drives up in the patrol car and whisks him away. As they leave, I feel sadness about his partner. I know that his partner must have experienced all kinds of carnage and destruction in his role as a Highway Patrol person. I wonder why this affected him so deeply. I think it might be the vastness of the destruction and devastation that really touched him deeply. After all, I realize that even Highway Patrol persons are also human.

I grab a Nutri-bar and a small bottle of orange juice for breakfast. Soon, it is 9 a.m. and time to drive to the bishop's meeting with the priests of our diocese in Biloxi. Obviously, we all have questions that need to be answered. The answers are not available and that leads to more frustration. Basically, we feel we are on our own and left to use our own resources and contacts to make things happen in and for our parishes.

While at the meeting, I get a call from CNN. They want to let me know they are in town. I let them know I will be back around noon.

I arrive back in Bay St. Louis and get ready for the rest of the day. Shortly afterward, the CNN crew arrives. I recognize Kathleen Koch, CNN's Washington Correspondent; from her days in the Bay St. Louis area when I served here in the mid-70's.

We enjoy the visit and interview during their almost two hour stay. It is wonderful reconnecting with her and finding out about all her sisters and brother and especially her parents. We tour the church; share some insights about deeper issues that the community and people will face down the road. When we finish with the interview, we both sit down at the table in my camper. Kathleen shares some of her experiences as she covered the initial report of the hurricane for CNN. She talks about her experience of visiting her old homestead on the beach and collecting some bricks for each member of her family. The home is now a pile of bricks and debris. She also talks about the volume of emails she received following her report. People were emailing her, asking her to try and find their loved ones for them. I begin to appreciate how covering the story became very personal for her and that, even though, she felt she needed to be objective; nevertheless, it became a very personal and heart-wrenching story for her.

Late this evening, amid all the running around and busyness, I discover that today is my fifth anniversary in Bay St. Louis. Little did I realize, five years ago, that I would be facing such a monumental task. In a way, I was reconnecting with the people of Bay St. Louis, some twenty-eight years later. Obviously, we all have changed. The Irish poet, William Butler Yeats comes to mind as I realize we have been changed, "changed utterly. A terrible beauty is born." I wonder about the beauty. It seems more like a terrible monster. Hopefully, a terrible beauty will be born inside me as well as in our community.

I remember when I was about to leave my former parish in Hattiesburg, Mississippi, someone with the gift of prophecy indicated that I would be "stretched." This must be part of it. But, how far can you stretch a person without that person breaking? Maybe, I will find out in the days and months ahead.

Another day. There is good news. The Power Company is hooking up the power to my temporary pole. There is more good news when the crane arrives to help with repairing the church roof. Work progresses on the temporary repairs to the church under the guidance and direction of Mike who is totally committed to the project. Beams are set in place and finally placing the tarp has begun.

The CNN crew arrives again to document the project of putting tarp on the roof. We chat for a while and take the camera crew upstairs so they can get a bird's eye view of the workers on the roof from their level.

There is a rumor floating around that, because of the immanent threat of Hurricane Rita to the Galveston-Houston area; that gas may be sidetracked to there for the emergency. People line up to buy gas, including myself.

Finally, there is a breather. Everyone seems to disappear. I ramble out to the BellSouth telephone bank and call my friend in Colorado—Mary Lou. I let her know that I have spent some time with her daughter, Kathleen the last two days as she works on a documentary for CNN. I update her on my situation and we close our conversation. I try to call my friends in Chicago and get an answering machine with my godchild's voice on it. Yesterday was her 14th birthday. I had some beautiful gifts set aside for her birthday before I went on vacation but Katrina came and stole them.

The day ends with another reconnecting experience. We discover that our church, even though battered, bruised and tarnished by Hurricane Katrina; it is still structurally sound. We receive the good news from the structural engineer, employed by the diocese. This is the best news we have received so far. Our people will be thrilled and excited when we share this good news with them this weekend at church.

This church stands as a beacon of hope for people in this community. Many of their lives are intertwined within its strong arms. They laugh and they cry here. They celebrate happy days and sad days here. They ask and pray here. They visit and form friendships here. They celebrate their comings and their goings here. Now, that we know that it can be salvaged, the link to the past through the present will continue into the future. Now, there is hope that will propel us into the future.

I wake the next morning to the sounds of persistent and heavy rain beating on the roof. The rain bands of Hurricane Rita are visiting us. I reach for my watch and it says 4 a.m. There is no point in getting up yet. I decide to lie there and just try and mix my own thoughts with the cacophony of the rain outside. As the rains beat heavily on the roof, my head is also filled with heavy thoughts. Again, there are more questions than answers. I go over the happenings of each day in my mind and try to relive them. There is no point in second guessing them. One makes whatever decisions one can at that moment with the resources one has at one's disposal at the time. This is not an ideal situation and we do not have the luxury of time to mull over things. Critical decisions have to be made at the moment and one has no choice but to live with them.

My mind fills with thoughts of the meeting I have to go to today at the diocese about our local school situation. I think of al kinds of scenarios that may be at play. I have been through my own hell with our elementary school these past five years. I have had to work with 5 different Principals during that time. Now, we have an excellent Principal, Janet, who has 27 years of involvement in Catholic education both as Principal and teacher. Her wisdom, commitment, dedication and loyalty to church and Catholic education cannot be undermined by anyone nor will I allow anyone to try and railroad her. She is too important to our school, community and its future growth and the families have rallied around her.

I have told her that she has my full support and that I will back her all the way. Our school and community has been through too much in recent years and now, especially, through Hurricane Katrina, we cannot afford to loose our identity.

I plan on going to that diocesan meeting ready to challenge our diocese and do what it takes to stand up for our school, its teachers and our students.

As a diocese, they know that they need me in this area. They need my direction, vision and presence to again build up the parish, schools and community. I know in my heart that I will support my community. We all have been through our own hell together and we will all resurrect together. Without my support, any major decisions they make will be ineffective.

It is time to get up—6:45 a.m. Mike is already up and ready for work. I get up and shower. It is nice to be able to have that luxury again. Now, it is time for a cup of hot tea. I haven't had one is almost a week and it tastes good even if I cannot put milk in it and have to contend with creamer. Two pop tarts also taste good and are enjoyable. A shave and a final clean up and I am ready for another day, to do battle with whatever obstacles come my way.

There is no point in driving back the 30 miles to Bay St. Louis this morning. I will stay around here and drive the 20 miles east to get to the meeting at 10 a.m.

I go outside just for some fresh air. The skies are dark and threatening. It is attempting to rain but cannot make up its mind but the wind reminds us who is in charge.

I head to Biloxi at 9:30 a.m. for the meeting. I arrive there a few minutes early. There are some people around and I chat with them. The bishop also drops by and concurs with the good news about the structure of our church. I tell him that the people will be thrilled with the news.

Finally, we head into the meeting. The meeting is frank and direct. Each pastor goes to bat for his own school and identity. The rest listen. The feelings will be brought to the bishop's attention.

I decide to connect with the past and go out to a nearby Wendy's for lunch. Obviously, there is no inside dining. Everyone is going through the drive-thru. I order my usual—#8 with honey mustard and a Sprite. I sit in the kitchen and eat it leisurely.

Once finished lunch, there isn't much more to do today, seeing that I cannot go to Bay St. Louis because of the weather. As I sit down to capture my thoughts, I find myself falling asleep. I realize the pressure I have been under the past 3 weeks and how my normal pattern of life has been totally disrupted. I know there will not be any normality for months, even years. The uncertainty is scary in one sense, but it challenges one to trust the Lord in a real sense; that He has one here for a reason and maybe we don't know the whole picture right now and, even if we did, we may not be able to handle it, so it is better to take one day at a time and we have no other choice.

Maybe, I need to get a cup of tea for myself. My usual routine before Katrina was to have a cup of tea at 3 in the afternoon, if I was home and we could share some down time with the rest of the staff in the kitchen. I need it.

A cup of tea and a rice crispy treat gets one back to former times and it is a welcome reprieve from the uncertainty of the present and future.

I feel housebound, not being able to go to Bay St. Louis today. I feel that I have not been productive. I know that Highway 603 into it was supposed to be closed because of rising waters in the bayous. Yet, part of me seems incomplete because I have not had a hands-on experience there today.

I try and keep busy sorting out the clutter in my SUV. Maybe it is a feeble attempt to organize and maybe it is also an escape from the boredom of not being where I feel I should be.

It is now 5 p.m. and the rain has ceased but the winds continue. We will see what the rest of the evening brings.

The next morning, two Krispy Kreme donuts and a cup of tea give me enough caffeine and sugar to kick-start another day.

As the day marches on, I realize that soon it will be time for evening Mass. People gather early and visit with each other. Some 70 people arrive which is double from last Saturday evening. During the Mass and homily, I speak about the fact that life seems unfair which is part of our first reading this evening. I share about how we all ask the question: why? And there is no easy answer. In our second reading, we hear how Jesus emptied himself to become one of us in order to redeem us. I share how we are being emptied right now through the exploits of the hurricane. We have been dispossessed and disconnected from ourselves, our belongings, our homes, our hearts and even our God. The gospel is about saying "yes" to someone and meaning it. It is the story of the man who asked his two sons to go out to work. One says "No" but changes his mind and goes; the other says he will go but doesn't go.

In the homily I try to give people hope; something to hold on to during these trying times. I can see heads nodding in agreement.

At the end of Mass, I update them on the status of our church and how our structural engineer said that the structure was okay. People all clap. It is an indication of how special and important this church is in their lives.

Following Mass, I decide to go to BellSouth phone bank and call my friend, Terry, in Chicago. I update her on what has happened since we last talked. She tells me about the project she is heading up in her parish for our school, especially our elementary school.

I wake up at 4 a.m. As I lie there, my thoughts are in the usual place—Hurricane Katrina. It is with me 24/7, even when I dream. This morning I even remember some of my dreams. They are about interviews with the press; glimpses of people's stories of heroism and the day to day happening that I have not had a chance to process fully.

I know it is Sunday and that Mike and Mary Ann are probably going to lie in this morning. They attended Mass last night. So, finally, I decide to get up, shower and shave.

I have my cup of hot tea and two honey buns and then it is time to head to Bay St. Louis. Even on a Sunday morning, the road is busy. There are power trucks on the way to another disaster as well as "relief convoys" on their way to some place else.

I arrive in Bay St. Louis and it is quiet there. I enjoy the peace and quiet for a change before all the people start to show up for Mass. Gradually, people arrive and visit. We are having the Mass in our Community Center again. The chairs are out but obviously not enough. Some people arrive with their collapsible chairs and cardboard fans to ward off the flies and stifling heat.

I make the same points I made last night in my homily. It has to be uplifting because these people have lost their heart as well as their belongings. I have no choice but to be upbeat. I integrate my thoughts with the readings and try and give people something to hold on to.

Toward the end, I share with them the progress of the week as well as some pending issues and, of course, the good news that our church is structurally okay. There is an outburst of applause from the 400+ congregation. It is a relief for them knowing that their church will continue and its beauty will be restored and preserved. I invite them to sign up if they need help in cleaning up their property from the volunteers who are waiting and willing to help.

Afterward, many people come forward and write down the kind of help they need. Most of it is clean up, removal of trees, etc. I will pass on the information and requests this week to the appropriate place.

I remind people that we will need lots of resources to rebuild our parish and community and that there are people here who have the gifts and knowledge we need. I invited them to step up to the plate and join us in restoring our parish and lives. We will need their expertise, their vision, their guidance and direction. I reminded them that the seminary did not offer a course on "how to rebuild after a hurricane."

Following Mass, people stay around and visit each other. No one is rushing off. It is nice to see people stopping, chatting and hugging each other; recognizing that each of them are alive.

I cannot stay in Bay St. Louis tonight. My "condo" is still in shelter because of the threat of Hurricane Rita. Maybe, tomorrow when I return to Bay St. Louis, George will have the camper, alias my "Condo," back in place and I will be able to, once again, reestablish a presence there.

Another Monday morning arrives and hopefully, it will not be filled with the "Monday morning blues." The day starts as usual with an early morning wake up. There is no need for an alarm clock. One's system is wired and programmed to react to another day. It is 5 a.m. and I am awake. I lie there, wondering is anyone going to get up. I keep checking my watch. Soon it is 6 a.m. and no one has ventured beyond the covers so I decide to do so. I make my way through the darkened halls to the bathroom where I confirm that I am alive and ready to face another day.

When I finish in the bathroom, Mike and Mary Ann surface and get ready for their day. A cup of hot tea and two honey buns provide my breakfast. Even thought the expiration date on the package is well past, I don't care. It is something quick and easy and I am ready to hit the road to Bay St. Louis.

I gas up again and head down Interstate 10 to Bay St. Louis. Traffic is pretty heavy at just after 7 in the morning but it is moving along well.

I reach the area where my rectory used to be and notice that George has brought back his camper again. This is good news. Now, I have my "condo" again. My first reaction is to see if the power is connected. Yes, it is and it is a nice surprise on a Monday morning. I tell George, who is still around, and he connects the power to the camper. It is great not to have to listen to a noisy generator all day and night again. Now, I can stay in my "condo" on a regular basis and maybe eventually be able to have a shower, especially if and when I get a FEMA trailer/camper.

Next I check the tarp on the church and see if it survived the remnants of Hurricane Rita. Yes, it did. This day is really off to a great start. Hopefully it will get better.

Yes, it does. Dan Wilkens arrives from Atlanta. Dan is coming to coordinate our volunteers for the next few months. He will become a tremendous blessing to our parish and our community. During the next few months, he will become the catalyst to help volunteers from around the country to connect with us and become reconnected with the whole concept of volunteerism.

It is now almost 9 a.m. and I have to call one of the reporters at "The Mayo News" newspaper in Ireland to update him on what has happened since I came back from vacation. I also remind him of the web site and tell him that he can use any pictures he wants. Hopefully, he will keep our needs before the people and the readers.

I receive a call from one of my classmates in New Jersey, Fr. Paddy. I update him on my situation. He tells me to hang in there and I will. I realize that this is the first time I talked to him since our class reunion in 1997. This is another opportunity to reconnect with former classmates.

John, from Home Depot, and his associate from Atlanta drop by with some more supplies especially a trailer for storage which is useful for storing the equipment we have received for cleaning, etc. He is very generous and willing to help with his resources and time. It is truly an inspiration.

As evening falls, people still come by and ask if there is anything they can do for us. They are so generous and genuine in their concern.

At around 6 p.m., I decide to check our the new feeding station. This one seems to be run by the Salvation Army. The line is a little long but people do not seem to mind. The food is pretty good: salad, hot dogs, hamburger or chicken and lemonade. I decide on the chicken and enjoy it.

Following supper, I decide to bring my laptop to the BellSouth phone bank and see if I can get connected to the Internet to check some of my emails. The connection is ancient history—7kb a second, and it takes forever. I email responses to two and decide, seeking that it is getting very hard and impossible to see the computer screen, to quit.

On the way home to my camper, "Condo", Jo, our parish secretary calls and updates me. She desperately wants to get her FEMA trailer and wants to have her own space. Who would not wish such at this stage.

The darkness envelopes me, and I am ready to call it a day. Maybe a bedtime reading might help as we close out another day.

It is another day, another morning as we awake to step into it in faith, not knowing what challenges and accomplishments may come our way.

I lie in bed wondering and waiting; knowing that one has to get up and face the day. It is 6:30 a.m. and I gather a change of clothes and head off to Jeanine's house about a ¼ mile away to get a shower. The door is open and I just walk in and hit the shower. There is no one around. It is a relief to be able to shower again, no matter how infrequently it may happen. I head back to shave and wash my face with some water from a bottle. We do not have water in the camper and one has to be creative and adjust to the situation.

I decide to head off to get some breakfast at the feeding place. The line is long, but it is still not too hot or humid yet, so we decide to join the line. It is moving very slowly. It seems the cooks cannot keep up with the demand but nobody seems to complain.

Conversations in the line gravitate toward the hurricane, naturally. People share stories and experiences. I listen in on some of the conversation. One worker tells of how he went to the home of an elderly lady yesterday to help her. She had diabetes and other ailments and needed help in recovery of her property and home. He tells how the elderly woman says that she had been faithful in paying her insurance premiums all the years. Now the insurance company is taking flight. She could not understand how; if she stood by the insurance company all the years, how they could not stand by her now in her time of need. What can one say to such a question?

Finally, I am ready to choose my breakfast. I decide on scrambled eggs, orange juice, frosted flakes. Of course, there are grits, but not for me. I want a fortified breakfast because I may not have the time or am willing to stand in line in the noonday heat for lunch. So I take an orange and a power bar just in case.

When I return to the church grounds, people are already at work in the church, clearing out and removing the floor and sub-floor. Jim, our maintenance person, is trying to connect water to the camper. Yes, it is another adventure in connecting and reconnecting with one of the essentials of our past—water. Yet, everything seems temporary right now but it is a step in the right direction.

Dan is back and has been talking with a FEMA representative from Washington. As we gathered along, what used to be the Beach Blvd., we are told that there are 24,000 homeless people in Hancock County, displaced by the hurricane. The authorities have run out of places to put trailers and have asked if we would make some of our property available to place trailers. FEMA would build the infrastructure needed. The parish would benefit in the long term from the infrastructure and the repairs they would make to the existing facilities. This would be a humanitarian gesture on our part to the people and we would love to do it. We do have some concerns about the details and time span. Mostly, we wonder if the bishop will give his approval.

Susan and her mother drop by for a visit. Susan drives from Tampa to help her mother clean up her house. Susan was a SEARCH team member with me years ago when I was Director of Youth for the diocese. SEARCH is a powerful youth to youth weekend retreat experience.

Obviously, there was no lunch today; just an orange and a power bar. Supper is no better now. Some Gatorade and another power bar. It is time to call it a night. Maybe, tomorrow, I will have a better opportunity to reconnect more with myself and my own inner journey.

It is an early morning once again. I awake at 5 a.m. and just lie in bed, thinking of what the day might bring as well as the small achievements we have accomplished so far.

I get up before 6 a.m.. I have a shower in my "condo" for the first time. This is a new experience. At least, I don't have to borrow a shower from someone else. I feel like a giant in a Lilliputian village. It is a crunching experience but tolerable. At least we do have hot water, thanks to George lighting the heater in the camper.

I decide that I will be early for breakfast this morning to beat the crowd and the long lines. I arrive there at 6:45 a.m. and wait in line. I am lucky to be the fifth person in line. This morning, we have some Mexican dish. I have no idea of its name but it is a welcome guest to a groaning stomach. We also have applesauce and orange juice. I discover that the companies who make the applesauce must have warehouses of it as it seems to be on the menu almost every day. Still, it all helps.

I sit down beside an elderly gentleman who just seems to want a captive audience and I am that one person audience. His name is Jesse. He tells me about his 5,000 book collection which is spared by the hurricane. His regret is that he has not a completely preserved Greek dictionary. As he speaks, he tells me about his studies in linguistics at a university in Hawaii and how he received his Master's in the U.S. I dare not ask him any questions because I will be held captive even longer. He excuses himself to get some salsa for his tortilla and I find a way to escape.

In the afternoon, I finally drive to the bank and deposit some money. I have never been to an outdoor bank before but there are lots of things I have never experienced before Hurricane Katrina. The outdoor bank is circled by armed guards. Eyes peel in different directions as they scan everyone who comes and goes. I also order some checks because I know there will be bills to pay.

Somehow, the Lord works in mysterious ways. I get a phone call from George in Minnesota. His parish is interested in helping out. He has the usual questions and they want to send down a truck load of supplies. I discourage him as we don't need them as such now. We need financial help. I suggest that his parish might sponsor a teacher. I hope this opens a door and, at least, another one of our teachers can remain. Obviously, her home is destroyed and she needs a job to help her, not only put her talents to use, but also to make the rebuilding process a little easier for her family.

As evening arrives, it gets quieter. Contract workers clock out for another day. A few sightseers drive slowly around, snapping pictures, fortified against the mud, muck and dust of the streets and parking lots.

I take one last stroll around the property and as I do. I hear the Red Cross announce, "hot meals" I rush up to get mine. No need to worry about what I might eat tonight. They took care of it.

I decide to take my laptop and head out to the BellSouth phone bank to download some emails. I get on my regular email address and find that I have hundreds of emails awaiting me. I go through the usual advertisement ones and delete them at once. There are too many other ones that I need to answer. I will have to go back tomorrow evening and try and answer some of them.

I arrive back and feel compelled to do one of my "Traveling Companion" columns on Hurricane Katrina. I decide on a title immediately and it is easy.—"She was no lady." In a few minutes I have an article written and will probably email it tomorrow to the editor of the paper.

Now, I can feel sleep beckoning and I must obey it. Tomorrow will be another day and we will see what surprises it brings.

Again, it is an early morning. I awake at 4 a.m. which is usual these days. There is no such thing as a schedule or routine anymore. I decide to get up at 5 a.m.; shower and shave and go to the portable toilet down the street. Seeing that the food kitchen at the ball park does not open until 7 a.m., I decide to walk along the beach. As I begin my journey, I can head the hissing of the electrical current in the wires overhead.

The beach is quiet. There are no people around, and no vehicles. The sun is just beginning to peek out from under its nighttime blanket. The waves gently roll ashore. It is quiet different when Katrina took charge some weeks ago.

Soon, it is time to head out and get a head start on the food line. We chat with some parishioners as we wait. A quick prayer of blessing and the line begins to move. This morning, it is scrambled egg; grits as usual, apple sauce and a choice of breakfast drinks. I also grab a box of Frosted Flakes to make sure I am fortified enough for the rest of the day. We sit down beside a group of our local police members and chat about the pressure and the need for days off.

Finishing breakfast, I head to the BellSouth phone bank and check emails at my regular email address. Last night, I deleted many of them that were just advertising. Today, I copy the ones I need to reply to and transfer them to a Word file. Maybe, later, I can email people. I do notice that some of my close friends have emailed me and I will try and call them later when I get a chance.

The afternoon is a buzz with activity. There are phone calls, visitors and interruptions. There is a phone call from Reggie in Fairhope, Alabama. He is bringing a group of 20 volunteers tomorrow for the weekend to help with clean up etc. They will be bringing a bobcat, a front-end loader and a grapple as well as chainsaws. We sure could use such equipment.

In the afternoon, I decide to go to the BellSouth phone bank and download some of the other emails as well as answer some. The connection speed is much better.

I also get the opportunity to call some dear friends, Guy and Mary in Phoenix. It has been a few years since we have been in touch. Guy sent me an email on August 31st wondering what had happened to me during the hurricane. The email said, "Mike. We are wondering about you following Hurricane Katrina? Please get in touch with us as soon as possible and let us know if you are okay." The email included a phone number to get in touch with him. Seeing that both of them were engaged in another conversation, we agreed to talk tomorrow morning.

When I arrive back, a contractor from out of town is waiting for me to see if I am ready to give him some work. I tell him that our own contractors will be our first choice for any construction we will be doing in the future. Obviously, he wants to leave his portfolio and calling card just in case we change our mind. Of course, we will not change our mind.

The next morning, I need to go to Sam's to get a printer. They open at 7 a.m. for business members. I qualify and head there. There are a few other shoppers there as I listen to the pep talks from headquarters over the PA system. Various people are receiving a pat on the back for their accomplishments but my thoughts are elsewhere.

I get my printer/scanner/copier combination and head to Bay St. Louis. I need to start sending "Thank you" letters to people who have contributed to our parish emergency fund.

Almost immediately, there is a phone call from MidWest Radio and the Tommy Marren. Show. They wish to do a live interview. It will necessitate being up at 4 a.m. on Monday morning. Being up at such time will not bother me as I am usually awake, if not up by then anyway. This will be 10 a.m. Irish time. This will provide a wonderful opportunity to update the audience in Ireland about what has happened since I got back.

Then, I am accosted by a reporter from "The Washington Times." He is doing a story on the relationship of faith to the hurricane. This is an interesting approach. I give him some sound bites to chew on. He has the courtesy to ask if it is okay to take pictures at our Sunday Mass. Exposure is important at this stage and we have to seize all the opportunities. The story will be in the Monday edition.

Later in the afternoon, I drop by the BellSouth phone bank and call Guy & Mary. Guy is at the hospital with Alexis who just had surgery. I talk to Mary at length about what is happening on the ground here. It is good to talk to her and help her understand the scope of the disaster here. I also talk with my brother, Tom, in Ireland, making him aware that I will be on MidWest radio on Monday morning.

Mary, our cook, comes and feeds all the workers here at lunchtime. She cooks one of her favorites—meatballs and spaghetti and, as usual, they were excellent.

Elaine, a teacher at our elementary school, along with her husband, drop by. She needs a hug. It has been tough for her. She lost her collection of over 30 years of teaching stuff. She wanted to see a picture of her classroom that I had taken and put on the Internet. Her tears were not far away as she spoke.

Janet, our elementary school principal calls. She wants to fill me in on what I have already heard from Sr. Jackie about the diocese's action in stopping all the cleanup on our schools. She is totally frustrated at the ineptitude of the diocese. They hire a group to come in and clean up the facility. They set a deadline for the school to restart and then they go and pull the rug out from under everyone who have been trying to meet the school's opening deadline.

It seems that everyone and no one is in charge at the diocese. This results in lack of leadership, direction and total frustration for those who are working in the field. What is the diocese going to say to parents who have been told that school will start on October 6th? The parents' frustration is at a very high level already. Who is going to explain to the parents what is happening? Why promises were broken? And will anyone take responsibility? I listen to the frustrations and despair of our principal and she feels she has been lied to and hung out to dry. This is going to have deep repercussions for a long time.

I can sense the same frustration from the priests I meet on a regular basis or who just drop by and share their frustrations. They are under tremendous pressure already and are getting no leadership or direction. They, too, feel they have been cut loose and left to their own resources. If priests ever get a chance to vent their frustrations at the lack of leadership, then it will be very interesting.

It is now almost 8 p.m., and it is time for supper—some leftover spaghetti and meatballs from earlier today. Then, I read for a while as I lie in the camper's bed. Finally, sleep visits and I accept the offer. Tomorrow is a different day. As I reflect on the past few days, I realize that I have encountered a series of reconnections and connections. The reconnections are very special in that I reconnected with some friends who got lost in my busyness. The connections are filled with new adventures where strangers, volunteers and many "anonymous" persons provide opportunities for ongoing friendships.

9

What Do You Say?

It is Sunday afternoon and there is a funeral this afternoon at 1 p.m. but this funeral is different. It is not the funeral of someone who had been sick for a long time and their death was expected. It is not the funeral of someone who had cancer and had finally succumbed to the disease. It is a funeral of a husband and wife who were drowned in Hurricane Katrina. Lukey and Gloria stayed in their home during the hurricane. During Hurricane Camille in 1969, they did not have water in their home. So, using Camille as a benchmark, they decided to stay in their own home for Hurricane Katrina. But Katrina was not as kind.

At least now, with the funeral taking place, their family can bring some kind of closure to the lives of their parents. They have waited five weeks for this day and I am sure the wait was painful. Finally, DMORT has released the remains of their parents and they can bury them.

Even though the funeral is scheduled for 1 p.m., many people keep coming and we are ready to start at 1:30 p.m.

During the past few days, I have agonized over what I should say at this funeral. What words of encouragement can I share? What hope can I give them? What answers do I have, if any?

As I ponder these weighty questions, I realize there are no easy answers. There is no quick-fix that will soothe the grief. There is no magical potion that will heal the pain. The questions outweigh the answers; the tears outweigh the hope; the loss outweighs the family solidarity. Yet, we gather to find some meaning; to look for some deeper purpose; to find some solace; to live in hope.

I know that, in the weeks ahead, I will face the same questions and struggles as I try to give some hope and provide some meaning and support for families who have lost loved ones in similar circumstances.

Weeks later, as Lukey and Carol's family celebrate Thanksgiving; DMORT drops another bombshell into their lives which explodes any closure they may have made on the death of their parents. DMORT informs them that they cremated the wrong person; that, instead of giving them the remains of their mother, they gave them the remains of someone else. What a Thanksgiving gift to receive, I think to myself. How much more can an agonizing family bear under these circumstances? Their lives have been devastated, not only by the hurricane but also by the death of their loved ones. Now, they have to participate in another nightmare that is not of their choice. DMORT asks them to bring the cremated remains of their "supposedly" mother to the local funeral home in exchange for the "real" remains of their mother. The remains of both are exchanged. The family, at the funeral home, are now ready to have a service for their "newly found" mother, while the family who thought they had had the funeral of their father and mother almost six weeks ago, can now bring this final saga to an end.

As the day wears on, my mind is still filled with overwhelming thoughts from the funeral today. I second-guess myself. Did I say the right thing? Did I give them hope? Did I really listen to their grief and their story? Did I allow God to work in and through me? My mind continues to fill with thoughts without readymade answers.

I need to go to bed soon as there is that 4 a.m. interview with Tommy M. on MidWest radio in the morning. I hope I will wake up in time to receive his call and that I can say the things and share the experiences here with the folks at home so they can help us some more.

Another day is almost ended. Another day on the road to recovery! Hopefully, progress has been made and it will continue.

Obviously, today, Monday, is going to be an early day. I awake early around 3 a.m. making sure that I did not miss the call from Tommy Marren of MidWest Radio in Ireland. The call comes around 4:05 a.m. and we chat for about 14 minutes. I update him on progress and how things have gone since my return from Ireland.

His questions are both interesting and perceptive. I had participated in a live radio interview with him the day before I returned from Ireland to the hell of Katrina.

Tommy's first question is obvious: "Is it much better or much worse than you expected when you went back from vacation? The answer is simple: it is much worse. Nothing can prepare you for the shock and overwhelming feeling you get when you first see the total devastation. You may have watched video of it on television; seen pictures on newspaper or through email; but, it is just a whimper compared to the avalanche of feelings you experience when you put your boots on the ground in the middle of the debris, stench and desolation for the first time. He asks about funerals and how does one cope or give people some words of encouragement. He also asks about feelings of anger and resentment from the people because the President and the government were so slow to respond to the crisis. I indicate to him that people have to find an outlet and an avenue to vent their frustrations and anger. Most often, they direct it at the inability of the government to respond. Finally, he asks about my own work as a priest; how different it is now compared to the normal day to day activities in a priest's life. I remind him that I see my role now as being there for people; to support them; to listen to their story; to allow them to cry on my shoulder and to give them hope.

After the interview, I pace up and down the sand strewn parking lot, wondering how the interview went. I wonder, did I say the right things? Will people get a real grasp of what has happened; what we are facing and whether or not we have the resources to rebuild our lives, homes and community. Yes, I wonder what else I could have said that I didn't say.

Seeing that it is still too early to go and find a breakfast place, I decide to go to the BellSouth phone bank and call home and see if they had any update or reaction to my interview with MidWest Radio earlier this morning. I also call my sister, Ann, in England to update her on things and keep in touch.

During the rest of the morning, I find myself asking, "What do you say? How do you react, advice, encourage, and support a troubled self and a troubled people?

What do you say when the person who loaned you your "condo" camper arrives and tells you that it is "condemned?" Of course, you have no idea what to say. You are totally dumbfounded. You wonder if "Murphy" is playing another trick on you with one of his laws! Yes, George—who loaned me his camper initially—had his insurance agent come by to evaluate the camper. It had survived Hurricane Katrina by George's home. It looked fine to me but I didn't have the critical eye of an insurance agent.

It is now 2 p.m. There is the rustle of people outside. I go out to investigate. George, who owns my "condo," is there. He has two men with him. It cannot be but it is. They have come to take away my "condemned" condo. We plead for a period of mourning. They feel sorry for us. They said they will come back again on Thursday. So, at least, we have two days to get all our stuff out of the camper and get ready to lose it.

I have visions of waking up in the early morning in bed, being whisked down the highway behind some pickup truck, cruising off to some junkyard and oblivion. I hope it does not become reality.

Maybe, I might get lucky and get my FEMA trailer before my condemned "condo" leaves. Could I be so lucky!

It is another early morning but that is nothing new. I think it is Thursday. It is 4 a.m. and I am ready to get up. But it is still dark outside and I just lie there and reflect on the fact that I have probably spend the last night in my "condo." Today is the day they are supposed to come and take it away. At least, they did not come while I was asleep and have me roll down the road in a bed at the back of a pick-up truck. That would be some story.

I finally decide to get up and shower and do the necessary grooming. Then, at 6 a.m., it is off to the BellSouth phone bank to check and answer some emails. It is still dark when I get there and connected. I am just a lone stranger connecting to the world at that particular place. I have a hard time seeing the keys on the keyboard because of the darkness but I manage. I do it from feel and connect. Once I have answered all the emails, I decide to call home and update them on what has happened since we last talked. They were surprised that I was calling so early in the morning.

I arrive back and Dan, our Volunteer Coordinator, is plodding the day. The project for today is to tear down the old frame building, used by Our Lady Academy and to demolish the rectory as well. We plod how we might be able to get it down without incurring any cost. Heavy equipment is at the ready at both places, waiting for the go-ahead. We wait and wait and wait but nothing seems to happen.

I spend most of the morning cleaning out the camper, putting all my belongings into the SUV which will become my traveling "suitcase" for a while. We unplug the water and the power and leave the "condo" to die a slow death.

Finally, there is movement. The company doing the clean up of the school agrees to pay for the demolition of the old frame building. Soon, the machine moves in and its giant claws begin to crush the frame building. People, who attended school there, stand around with cameras and begin the mourning period as they see the first beams crushed into crumbs of timbers. History has been made and a new era begins. Finally, all that remains is a huge pile of broken memories and experience in the form of a pile of thrashed lumber and galvanize. Former students have their private moments. I even notice some tears slip down ready cheeks as memories of school days and experiences, flood minds and bodies that were formed there in a former era. What does one say? There is nothing to see; only space and time to grasp and come to terms with history being remade. Then everyone goes home to ponder what they just witnessed.

While they were crushing the old frame building, I glanced away to see a pick up truck pulling away with my "condo" camper. I had thoughts of getting a final picture of it but they sped down the street into oblivion.

Now, it is evening. I had hoped that I might receive my FEMA trailer today. I kept anticipating that phone call but it never came. I thought I was logical. Jo, our secretary, had received a visit from FEMA on Sunday morning and got her trailer, yesterday (Wednesday). Logically, I got a visit from FEMA on Monday and so I anticipated getting the trailer today. But, then again, many times, government often defies logic. What do I say to myself? I have no choice but to live in hope and I will for some, not-too-distant, day.

There is no point in hanging around Bay St. Louis. My "condo" has gone to its own graveyard. So I head to BellSouth phone bank to check and answer some emails. As it is getting dark, I head to Gulfport and to Mike & Mary Ann's in Gulfport for the night.

It is quiet when I arrive as they are out. I decide to make myself a cup of tea. It's been a long time since I had one and I read the local papers which, now, has become a novelty. Soon, they arrive back and we settle for spaghetti and sauce. Some time later, an air mattress calls and I respond.

The next day brings more discoveries and raw feelings. I receive a call from Emily a CNN Producer, confirming the networks plans to visit with us over the weekend and to be ready for a more in-depth interview on Monday. Following the phone call, my mind goes into its questioning mode: What shall I say? What needs to be said? What does the rest of the world need to know about us right now? Are they just going to be looking for sound-bites? Are they going to be asking about the attitude and disposition of the people in the area? I try to anticipate the questions and formulate some possible answers.

Finally, the crew hired by FEMA to demolish the rectory arrives and strikes the first blow. I had called Jo, our secretary and Kathleen, our Pastoral Associate, to witness the destruction. They arrive just before the demolition begins. Of course, we have to take some pictures to capture this historic moment. We, as a parish staff, stand at a distance. Even though we are physically removed from the building; our minds and hearts are very much intertwined in the rubble. We reflect on stories shared and experiences lived within its offices and corridors. Our taste-buds relive the many fine meals we ate there under the watchful eye of Mary, our excellent cook. We think about the many visitors who dropped in to sample the same meals also. We remember the good times and the stresses that emanated from its hallowed halls. We think about the troubled souls who walked in the front-door, many times, unannounced, and looked for a trusting listener.

Now, all those experiences and memories, disturbed by an outreaching and merciless crushing arm; will sink deep into our psyches. We hope that, one day, we will be able to sort through this mental debris and maybe retool it for the journey ahead. Yes, what more does one say? Maybe, much more but that too can wait.

As evening closed in, the demolition crew has to stop and wait for another day to finish the job.

I receive a phone call from the local funeral home to indicate that I will have two funerals early next week—one of Monday and one on Tuesday. How do I prepare myself, psychologically, for them? What do I share that will, in some small way, lessen the pain?

At 6 p.m., I decide to journey to the BellSouth phone bank; check and answer some of my emails and travel on to Gulfport again tonight.

As I travel along Interstate 10, I can see a glorious sunset in my rear view mirror. I muse about the happenings of the day and savor the achievements and build up some hope for the future. Maybe, the good Lord is using the sunset to remind me to live in hope for a sunrise.

Obviously, what I waited for didn't happen. I didn't get my trailer from FEMA today either. Maybe, I will get it tomorrow. One has to live in hope and have something to look forward to. At least, hopefully, I will have the 12 X 60 foot trailer this coming week. I really appreciate the tireless energy and determination of Eileen in Orlando who never gave up on the prospect of getting me a trailer for a parish office.

A cup of tea and some homemade brownies give me the energy to stop and write down my thoughts for today. At this time of the evening, it is difficult staying awake but a cup of tea provides me with enough energy to finalize my thoughts for the day.

Tomorrow is another day and I will try to embrace it in hope and expectation. Maybe, some achievements will be thrown into my lap and maybe, just maybe, there might be a visit from FEMA with a trailer. Until tomorrow, a restful night and enough energy to face another day in the hell of Katrina's aftermath.

It is 4 a.m. on Saturday morning and I am wide awake. I just lie there in anticipation of the day ahead. I know that Mike and Mary Ann need to sleep in this morning so I finally decide to get up at 5:30; shower, shave and do the other morning rituals before breakfast. Breakfast is simple and quick—a cup of hot tea and two pop-up tarts. Then it is time to get ready for another day in Bay St. Louis. First, I need to get some gas for my gas guzzler. I pull up, put in my Shell MasterCard and it gets rejected. The gas pump tells me to "ask the cashier." I ask her and she informs me that the card is rejected. I think I know why and who the culprit is. Her name is Katrina. Obviously, my September bill did not get paid because of the hurricane and so Chase Bank decided to close the card so I could not make any further purchases of gas on it. This is just another one of the frustrations one has to deal with. What does one say? It is just another problem in the myriad of daily problems. I know what I need to do to solve it and I will, amid the many frustrations that Katrina brought with her.

Our first major obstacle today is the try and get the rest of the rectory demolished and taken away. Everything goes fine for a while until Cindy arrives and tells us "there is a problem." We all scurry around to find out what the problem might be. The Corps of Engineers as well as FEMA representatives arrive and we have a series of mini meetings to see if we can iron out the problem. Basically, we are told that FEMA is willing to help us get rid of the debris but, now we are engaged in "demolition" which FEMA does not support. Obviously, some people want to go into the finer points, while others, want to deal with it, practically. Your guess who won!—the finer points. In the meantime, we come up with some creative ways on our own that will and eventually did take care of our main goal—knock down the remaining structure of the rectory and have it hauled away at the same time. What do you say when two agencies are more interested in the finer points while everything else is a mess around them? Do we debate nuances or engage in practicality?

I notice a cavalcade of Highway Patrol cars coming down along the beach and turning on to Union St. next door. Then I receive a phone call from one of the reporters from the SunHerald newspaper, informing me that the elder President Bush is in town and passing by. The reporter asks if I am interested in going to the Fire Department to see the former President. I tell him that I will be glad to have the President drop by our church. The conversation ends. I am more excited about meeting some people at church later this evening that in meeting a former President of the United States. The big picture is much bigger than even the President and I know I have to keep that in mind.

It is Sunday morning again. This morning, we decide to have an extra morning Mass at 8 a.m., in anticipation of more parishioners returning to the community.

Shortly after I arrive, Brian R. the CNN producer from Washington, arrives. He is the main producer of the one-hour documentary on the recovery of Bay St. Louis after Hurricane Katrina. We walk around and chat before Mass.

People begin arriving for the 10:30 a.m. Mass and we anticipate the arrival of the bishop. It seems the bishop has been visiting various communities affected by Hurricane Katrina to offer support. The crowds begin to gather—more than last week. People even arrive with their own folding chairs. The majority of people stand as there are not enough chairs.

Mass begins with the bishop as the main celebrant. Most protocols are observed until the end when I update the people on the progress we have made since last week. I ask if there are any questions. I get some and then Pam fires a question to the bishop about how much the Vatican has been involved? The bishop answers it and then dances around it, according to some later comments.

The bishop reminds the people about the wonderful job I am doing as their pastor. It is a regular occurrence when he visits any parish. What humbles me is the standing ovation the people give me. I feel embarrassed and overwhelmed. I know they need strong and courageous leadership at this time; someone who will give them hope and knit them together again as a community and I am the one who has been chosen to do it. It is a monumental task and can be overwhelming. But if the Lord put me in this situation, then I know he will give me the resources needed to make it happen.

I receive and accept a luncheon invitation to Myrt's place—at least, the front lawn of what used to be her once proud home on the beach. We eat fried chicken, drink lukewarm water and munch on peanut butter cookies.

As we stand around the makeshift table as a group of adults, I notice the children prancing through the ruins of Myrt and Mike's house. I wonder what they might be thinking. Are they engaged in a treasure hunt? Deep down, what is going on inside those childlike but impressionable minds? Can they absorb the implications of what they are dancing through? Is it an exercise in discovery or escape? I wonder!

When I arrive back, later that evening, I find the group of our volunteers gathered around a scented candle. They are chatting and sharing some stories. Someone has brought them some gumbo and they are really enjoying it. What really strikes me is the friendship that has developed among people from diverse backgrounds and areas of the country. It is interesting how a catastrophe brings together an unlikely cast of characters and turns them into real buddies.

Finally, Bill and Bill Jr. say "good night" to everyone who will be leaving for home at 2 a.m. and don't want to disturb anyone. There are genuine promises to keep in touch and even a few tears are shed.

Another day! Another early morning! Another day to wait in hope! I awake at 4 a.m. as usual. I am wondering when I will be able to take out my new bike out for a ride again along the beach. Thanks to Chuck in Houston, I have pedal power again. But, all that will have to wait for another day.

A quick visit to the portable toilets and then off to Jenise's for a quick shower and back for a shave and other morning chores and we are ready for another day and week.

Dan, our Volunteer Coordinator, has the crew busy working on cleaning the slab where the rectory once sat. We are secretly hoping that the FEMA trailer might come today so we wait in hope.

I stop by the elementary school to see what progress, if any has been made, since last night. Some progress has been made, especially in the laying of the tiles. While there, several parishioners stop by and make comments on the Mass with the bishop yesterday. The comments are both interesting and insightful. One person remarks on the contrast between the pastor and the bishop. The bishop was impeccable dressed, white shirt, cuff-links, not a hair out of place. They said, I looked ragged, sunburned, hair all over the place. Then they said that if they needed someone when they were in trouble, they would choose someone who was in the trenches.

Some of the other comments later in the day are also interesting. One person says that the bishop seemed afraid, was not comfortable, felt overwhelmed and even removed from the situation. It is interesting to listen to the comments of some of the lay people as well as recognize their candor in speaking their thoughts and feelings.

We enjoy a hamburger, cold slaw and beans for lunch and wash them down with cold water. Then, it is off to perform an afternoon funeral at the funeral home and then to the cemetery. Again, I am faced with sharing some thoughts that might give the mourners hope. I realize I need to hear the same thoughts myself. This is the first time I dress in my black pants and black shirt. I have to dethrone my hurricane ware for it. Following my part of the service, the American Legion and the Masons conduct their services.

I return from the funeral shortly after 3 p.m. in time to meet the CNN crew. Some of the crew had been here before and yesterday, I had the privilege of meeting Brian, the Producer of the documentary, for the first time. We conduct the interview standing in the parking lot by the old rectory. I have been giving a lot of thought to this interview. I know I need to share more than pithy sound bites. I need to share how grateful we are for the "outside" help; especially the countless number of volunteers to came to help us and continue to come. I need to try and capture the mood of the area since the hurricane; how people are coping; what lies ahead; some of the psychological issues that are surfacing presently as well as indicate the resilience of the people who have been through the hurricane. The interview lasts about ninety minutes. I'm sure they will have lots of editing and I am hoping they will. I enjoy doing it as I share some personal reflections and some hopes for the community and people.

During the interview, I can see the Red Cross truck drive by with hot meals. I wish I could break away and get some for the group of volunteers here but that is not possible. We will have to find other alternative sources for food this evening.

I receive a phone call from Betty. She has been trying to find out if a real "condo" might be available for me at Diamondhead. She calls with good news. There is one available and it will be ready by tomorrow afternoon. Seeing that my trailer from FEMA has not arrived yet, I have no choice but to avail of this opportunity. Tonight, I will probably spend well, in hope and anticipation.

Later in the evening, I take my laptop to the BellSouth phone bank to check and answer some emails. When I arrive there, it seems none of the laptop connections are working except one and there is a lady there with her laptop on line. I hang around for a while to see if she might finish soon but indications are she will not, so I leave.

When I arrive back, the volunteers have already eaten but have kept a dinner warm for me. I eat it and we just sit around and share some stories like the evening before.

Soon, little by little, folks go off to have a cold shower in the gym of Our Lady Academy. They are grateful for such after a hard day of labor.

It is close to 9 p.m. and we gradually disappear into our nocturnal abodes for well earned rest.

Tuesday morning, I awake at the usual early hour and just lie there anticipating and planning for the day that is just dawning, even with any surprises it may throw at me.

At 6:15 a.m. I head out to Jeanine's to take a shower. I know she is up early. She is there doing some early morning chores and I breeze in to have a quick shower to start the day. Then it is on to the BellSouth phone bank to check some emails. While there, I also call my sister, Ann, in England to update her on what has been happening.

Once I check emails and answer some, I head off to the usual feeding place. There is no line as it is just after 7 a.m. and I get my usual fortifications for the day—we have bacon strips, scrambled eggs, grits which I bypass, watermelon and of course, cereal. The choice of drinks includes Gatorade. Even though it is watered down severely, I still indulge. It may still give me energy for the day. I grab a few bars of peanut butter to take back to the volunteers and we are ready for another energy-filled day.

Kathleen K., the CNN Washington Correspondent, calls and wants to come with her daughters to work and experience the devastation. One of the parents informs me that I featured on CCN news earlier this morning. They must have broadcast a segment of my interview from a few days ago.

Jo, our secretary, arrives to take care of some business for the parish as well as the collection. She suggests that we get po-boys for lunch and we finally get them after a considerable delay. Still, they are welcome and good.

Later in the afternoon, I decide to go and check out my new "Condo" in Diamondhead. I collect the key and walk into my one-bedroom palace and can't believe how lucky I am. I will be able to sleep in a real bed, shower in a real shower and do my morning ablutions in a real bathroom. I will be able to use it until November 1st.

When I arrive back from Diamondhead, Eileen arrives with her 4 year old daughter from Orlando. She has brought some school supplies for our elementary school. Eileen is the one who has been persistent in having me registered with FEMA and she has also procured the large trailer that will be used as office space. We are living in hope that it will arrive soon.

Tony has invited the volunteer group to a house where he is cooking supper and we arrive there around 6 p.m. We are treated to a royal feast with mashed potatoes, ham, roast, salad, peas, corn, bread and butterscotch pudding for dessert. I feel like royalty, having my first "real" meal in almost six weeks. Maybe, it will help stop my weight erosion. After all, I cannot afford to lose any, nor do I need extra insulation. Hungry tummies are happy and I leave to head back to Diamondhead to experience my first night in my new "Condo."

On the way there, I get some gas and head to the Condo Village. I decide to soak all my weary bones in a hot bath and enjoy myself for a few minutes of real comfort. There is no TV, at least no cable, so I decide to go to bed and anticipate enjoying my first night sleeping on a real bed. As I do, I realize I have not watched any television since I arrived back from vacation, some six weeks ago. I really do not miss it. I do not need it as a distraction. I can manufacture my own and they are more personal. Maybe, I am missing some "breaking story" somewhere in the world but, then again, all I have to do is to look deep inside myself at the broken pieces of my own developing story. Somehow, the larger world seems much smaller when compared to my own world and the debris-ridden world of our community members. The latest sports results; the Wall Street numbers; the impending store sales and the so-called "favorite" TV shows have disappeared from my mind's radar screen. They have been replaced by my own "reality show" which is much more real that any of the fabricated ones on television.

It is Wednesday morning and it feels like I died and went to heaven. I awake from my first night's sleep in a real bed. I just lie there for a while and soak in the thoughts and experiences that flood my mind. I participate in the usual morning rituals before leaving. A breakfast of toast and tea is a fitting beginning to the day. I notice the condo also has a washer and dryer. Obviously, I will be making full use of its gifts in the days ahead.

It is now 6 a.m. and time to head back to Bay St. Louis. The traffic is pretty heavy on the way and it is still dark. I decide to go to the BellSouth phone bank to check emails and respond to others. While there, I also do some research on a Dell computer system for Jo, our parish secretary and make my decision.

As I am walking around, I notice a group who have been operating out of the local Methodist Church. One member of the group is Catholic. She mentions that it is interesting that most religious denominations have teams of workers and volunteers in the area but wonders where the Catholic groups are. Her comments are very interesting. She mention that she had called Catholic Charities and wanted to volunteer. She was told that they were not accepting volunteers, just donations. I tell her that we have some Catholic volunteers working with us and also give her some information on our special Hurricane Katrina web site. As they leave, my mind begins to whirl into overdrive and I ask myself: what do you say to people when they ask you—where are the Catholic volunteers? I sit down at my laptop and allow the thoughts to flow. It forms the basis for one of my upcoming articles in "Gulf Pine Catholic," our Diocesan newspaper.

A group of Methodist volunteers stopped by a few weeks ago. They were also helping at the local Methodist Church. Mary introduced herself as Catholic from California. She had left California a week earlier, hoping to find some Catholic group to do volunteer work in the aftermath of Hurricane Katrina. She called the national Catholic Charities office and asked about volunteering and was told, "We are not taking volunteers. We are only taking money." Undaunted by the response, she contacted the local Methodist Church and was put in contact immediately with a Methodist group working in the Bay St. Louis area. She was totally dismayed at the lack of cooperation and response from the Catholic Church as far as volunteers were concerned.

In recent weeks, I have heard and seen the same scenario played out hundreds of times. My parishioners have asked hundreds of times: "Where are the Catholic volunteers?" They indicate that there seems to be no groups of Catholic volunteers working in the area. They remind me that they have depended on Baptist,

Methodist, Mormon, Pentecostal, Presbyterian and other denominations to single-handedly clean out their homes. They also remind me that the presence of non-Catholic groups working in the area is obvious. Their disaster relief conveys are everywhere. Their feeding stations are dotted around the place. Their supply and staging centers are very noticeable and prominent.

Many of our parishioners have experienced a group called "Samaritans Purse." The group, under the auspices of Franklin Graham, son of the famous Billy Graham; mucked out houses, took out sheetrock and disinfected them. They were even conscious of people's possessions and memories. They walked with children through the debris and allowed them to talk about their experiences and help begin the healing process for them.

My parishioners still ask: "Where are the Catholic volunteers?' I do not have an answer for them. In fact, the absence of identifiable Catholic volunteers is obvious to the people suffering most from the hurricane.

Yesterday, a young woman who is very active in the church and school stopped by to chat with me. She shared her frustration with the national Catholic Charities organization where she had been continually stonewalled in any efforts to enlist help. They finally sent her a "Needs Assessment and Work Request Form." She commented that it was too late and wondered where the organization was earlier when the needs were obvious. She also mentioned that other church groups didn't send forms for people to fill out. Instead, they sent teams of people who actually cleaned out people's homes of the mud, mold, sheetrock and debris.

This morning, I noticed a Baptist Disaster Team from Tampa, Florida, pass by as I was doing my car line duty at our elementary school. I thought it was rather ironic.

I think about the volunteers who are helping our parish clean up and help us in the rebuilding process. Individual parishes in Wisconsin, Georgia and Mississippi send volunteers to help us. We initiated the contacts ourselves. But we have had large groups from non-Catholic churches and universities in various places arrive with heavy equipment to help us with the cleanup process.

Catholic Charities gave 3 million dollars to our diocese which is wonderful. Obviously, it is an indication of the generosity of people around the country.

At a time of disaster, such as Hurricane Katrina, visibility and action are not only a priority but a necessity. The greatest witness is for church volunteers to be working at the grassroots, immersed in the lives and struggles of the people most affected. From a grassroots perspective, people will continue to ask and wonder: 'where are the Catholic volunteers?'"

I know that this article will disturb some people out of their comfortableness. I know they will say that I do not have all the information. They will probably say I am misguided that I am suffering from post Hurricane Katrina stress. They may try and bruise the messenger but the message will be able to stand on its own feet and provide an opportunity for everyone to examine their consciences. In the end, it boils down to that same often repeated question: "What do you say?"

10

You Say, "I do."

It is Saturday and it is big day of Natalie and Jason. Today, they will exchange vows. Obviously, the wedding cannot be performed inside the church because of the destruction within it. Instead, it takes place on the front steps of the church, between the giant columns that, hopefully, will protect them against any metaphorical hurricanes in their married life. They are nervous but somewhat relaxed. In blazing sunshine, invited guests are seated on metal chairs around the horseshoe driveway of the church. Maybe, it is ironic that a horseshoe is also a sign of luck. The white runner guides its way up the steps where two kneelers await the promising couple.

Earlier in the day, some volunteers cleaned the area. Also, they have roped off special areas so that no one, other than the wedding guests, could enter. They want to make it special for both Natalie and Jason. After all, this is the first wedding to be held at the church following Hurricane Katrina.

There is an excitement and anticipation in the air. Even a photographer from "The Washington Times" arrives back especially to photograph the wedding, for his newspaper as well as donate a series of his pictures to the bride and groom.

Following the wedding, we gather at Jason's parent's home for a special celebration in the backyard, shaded by overhanging trees.

It is almost 4:30 p.m. and we just got word that the office trailer, courtesy of West Orlando Rotary Club, is almost here. Shortly afterwards, we notice the office trailer making the turn onto the Beach from Washington St. Everyone is getting exited, especially our secretary, Jo. Now, she will have a place she can call an office on a more permanent basis than before. Gradually, we usher it onto the slab where once sat the rectory. A quick glance inside shows how spacious this trailer is. It is almost 60 foot long and 12 foot wide. Inside, it is bare. There are two offices on either end and in the middle a handicapped bathroom and an open space for another office. It is bereft of furniture so we will have to go begging for furniture. We realize when Eileen, our friend in Orlando said, she would; now we know she did and followed up on her commitment.

Soon it is time for evening Mass. We have a larger crowd that the week before which is good because it indicates than more and more people are coming back on a more regular basis.

Our first reading shares the story of King Cyrus, chosen by God to lead the people from captivity in Babylon. I help the folks to try and relate to their own situation; how they may find themselves in situations and places they didn't plan but were meant to be. We meet a God who not only says "I do" but follows through in releasing his people from slavery in Babylon. We hope and pray that this same God will release the people affected from the destruction of Katrina and help them have a fresh start.

Later that evening. We say "goodbye" to the group from Wisconsin who came to help us. They have lifted our spirits and have shared their gifts and talents with us. They have been true to their word and have shown it in action.

Another group joins us this weekend. We have a group of forty students and faculty members from Elon University in North Carolina. They have pitched their tents by the beach and receive a wonderful wake-up call from a spectacular sunrise. Following Mass, they provide lunch for the people attending Mass.

Also, people from the University of Virginia arrive with very practical help. They bring cleaning supplies; rakes, shovels, garbage cans, wheelbarrows, toiletries and some clothes. People appreciate the practical nature of their gifts. It is inspiring to witness the dedication, commitment and hard work of these college students.

Following Mass, we baptize Brennan and he sure didn't like it. He cried through the whole service. Again, we are fortunate to see his parents witness to their own faith and making a commitment to share it with Brennan as he grows up.

Monday morning begins another week and we anticipate some more commitments. The electrical contractors who are working on the church arrive and we get them to erect a temporary pole and power so we can have electricity in our office trailer.

I get a phone call from "The Irish Echo" in New York and Ray, one of the reporters, wants to do a special drive for us under the auspices of the Ancient Order of Hibernians. He also has connections with the area here which makes it more personal. It seems the Mayomen's Association in Cleveland contacted the newspaper to enlist their help. It is amazing how the communications and enthusiasm as well as dedication spreads. Again, I am grateful for the vast network of individuals and groups who commit to help us in the recovery process.

This evening, we are invited by Dick and Bonnie to dine with them in their RV. Dick and Bonnie are from Cape Cod, in Massachusetts. They are both retired and are making a whirlwind tour across the United States. A few days ago, they called us, indicating they would be willing to help us for a few weeks. Gladly, we accept the offer. Before I do, I have to do an interview with one of the journalism students from Elon University for their newspaper.

The dinner is excellent. We have steak, grilled by Dick, cold slaw, string beans and a choice of drinks, including wine. Following supper, we decided to watch St. Stanislaus video of Hurricane Katrina on DVD and all were amazed at the ferocity of the hurricane as it lashed its way inland. We reflect on the vicious nature of the hurricane, but are also grateful for people like Dick and Bonnie who commit themselves to us for a few weeks.

The next morning, the group from Elon University are about to leave. I stop by the group and Dan is giving them some last minute thoughts. I put together my own thoughts, reminding them that their contribution to the community this weekend will not go unnoticed. I remind them that they have changed because of their experience here with us and that we have also changed because of what they brought to our community. We invite them back any time, especially for our July 4th weekend Crab Fest when we will celebrate, as a community, our recovery to that point.

My friend, Terry from Chicago calls to let me know about some of the roadblocks she is experiencing in getting her parish to commit to supporting us. She is not giving up. I have known the family for years and we have been good friends. I update her on all that has been happening here. She also mentioned that she and John were interested in coming down for a long weekend. I encouraged them. Again, I am amazed and humbled by the sheer determination and commitment of people who wish to help.

Later in the afternoon, I receive a phone call from Carolyn in S. Dakota She is wondering how things are going. She mentions that they will be in the area in mid-November and I encourage them to come and visit with us. Carolyn and her husband, Bill, have been friends for over seventeen years and I treasure their friendship, their loyalty and their support.

Wednesday morning greets me at 3:30 a.m. and I am awake. As usual, I lie there and try to go back to sleep but it doesn't visit me. Finally, I get up at 5 a.m. and do the usual morning chores. Breakfast is simple—some cereal and some hot tea. Then it is time, in the dark, to head back to Bay St. Louis again.

As usual, I stop off at the "hot spot" to check my email and respond, as well as check some home news stories. On the way, I wait in line to get some gas and head to the church parking lot.

My usual routine this morning is to go to the car line at our elementary school to meet the kids and parents for another school day. It is cooler this morning, so I wear a sweater for a change. Prior to Hurricane Katrina, this was also my usual routine. I feel compelled to continue it in order to have some connection with the past.

I have a meeting at 8:30 with some diocesan officials about insurance and the cost of clean up of the school, especially the high school. We are told that clean up work has been halted on the high school. This is just another one of the frustrations we continue to encounter along the way.

The meeting is very tense at times as we ask some very direct questions and do not get the answers we would like. We are told we will. Seeing that we have no idea of how much we will get in insurance, we cannot plan for anything. There are so many unknowns. We are expected to rebuild but we have no idea of what our financial base will be to start from. The whole experience is frustrating in that I discover that some "I do's" become "I can't."

Some FEMA contractors arrive, wondering where Jim, our maintenance man's trailer, is going to be placed. They install a pole for electricity and leave. Minutes later, we receive a call from FEMA, indicting that Janet's—our Elementary School Principal—trailer is being delivered. Shortly, afterwards, it arrives and is set up. Janet arrives to inspect it. It seems to be a very nice trailer and we hope she enjoys it. We, also, hope that we will have our own trailer to live in some day in the very near future. We continue to live in hope and pray that someone's "I do" will become "I did."

The next morning, I awake at the usual time and finally exit bed and do the usual morning chores before heading to Bay St. Louis. A simple breakfast of orange juice and toast has to suffice because the milk is sour and so there is no cereal this morning.

It is just after 6 a.m. and the ride to Bay St. Louis is shrouded in fog. I hope this is not an omen of what the day is going to be like. I pierce my way through the fog to find the "hot spot" to check emails and find out the email addresses and phone numbers of some of the software companies we had been using personally and in the parish. Later, we will call some of those software companies and see if they will replace our lost, original disks. Some indicate they will. Others claim it is our misfortune and ask that we purchase a new set. At least, we appreciate the courtesy and understanding of the companies who wish to help and we decide to cut ties with those who decline.

We receive a call from the diocese about the ongoing saga at Our Lady Academy and the clean up crew they initially hired. They seem to have resolved the issue and so, at least, Our Lady Academy High School can begin as planned.

Lunch, courtesy of the Red Cross, is hot dogs and chili and was eat at the elementary school cafeteria where they also served lunch to the children.

Some folks from the U.S. Department of Commerce come by. Supposedly, they are checking out why some buildings didn't make it through the hurricane. The volunteers here are not too impressed with their job description and feel that government money could be spent much more wisely, seeing that two other gentlemen from the same group were here yesterday doing the same thing. They just perform a cursory examination of our church structure. We wonder what advice that same church would give them, seeing that it has survived three hurricanes so far. But, then again, they are doing their job and if their recommendations will help in future planning, maybe, the whole experience will be worthwhile.

After lunch the next day, a FEMA trailer arrives. Obviously, it is not for me. This time it is for Jim, our maintenance man. I am still waiting even though I applied weeks before Jim and the others on our slab at present. Anyway, this is no time to be miserable. There is a wedding this afternoon. I need to change into my more formal attire for it and head out there in the sunshine to witness the marriage of Johnny and Jamie. I notice the photographer, Jimmy, taking pictures of the bridal party in the ruins of the church and even down in the foundation. It might seem providential and interesting. I realize that, from the bowels of this earth, will arise hope and prayer.

The wedding begins just after 2:30 p.m. A gentle breeze caresses the people as the couple stand in the shade between the porticos of the entryway to the church. There is a relaxed atmosphere and a naturalness to the whole process. God's gifts and blessings are with them on their married life journey.

Following the wedding, we attend the reception in the backyard of Jamie's home. It is very relaxed and cordial and the food is both good and Italian. Some time later, we leave to get prepared for evening Mass.

This evening, we have a bigger than normal crowd at Mass. It is an indication of more and more people coming. I also remind them that we hope to begin morning Mass soon so we can continue some routine in the parish.

Today is Sunday, October 23rd. Today is the first anniversary of my mother's death. It seems such a short year and so many things have happened, especially how our comfort zone has been totally destroyed by the hurricane. As I reflect on the anniversary, I am grateful for many things. I am grateful especially, in the light of the hurricane, that she was not alive when the hurricane happened because she could not handle the thought of me having to return to the chaos after the hurricane. Maybe, the Lord knew what he was doing in more ways than one—first of all, in sparing her the agony of having to deal with my returning to the aftermath of the hurricane and secondly and more personally, the fact that I was on vacation when the hurricane happened. I know that if I had been here, I probably would have stayed in the rectory because it was supposed to be hurricane proof and if I did stay there, I would be lying under the fresh sod somewhere. Yes, the Lord knew what he was doing and obviously, he has me in this situation for a reason and placed upon my shoulders the burden of rebuilding our parish and our faith community and helping the people grow strong again at their broken places. I hope and pray I am up to the task set before me. Maybe, if the Lord has a plan and a place for me in all this hurricane aftermath; then, too, he will not only open the doors to discover such but will also direct me through such doors.

It's early morning again. After lying awake in bed for a while, I salute the day and prepare for it with the usual morning chores at 5:30 a.m. Breakfast is again simple—toast and orange juice. Milk would be a welcome guest and I will try today and get some. At 6:30 a.m. I am heading south to Bay St. Louis in anticipation of meeting more people at Masses this morning. It is much cooler this morning and demands long pants and a sweater.

We had some extra folks at our 8 a.m. Mass this morning. It is good to see the folks coming back, even if it is a gradual process.

Soon, it is time for 10:30 a.m. Mass and the people begin to gather. As they do, more and more people I have not seen since the hurricane arrive. Mass goes on as usual.

Following Mass, a gentleman working with FEMA indicates that they will help me with a trailer. He gives me his name and phone number and asks me to call him tomorrow when he has access to a computer where he can check. Maybe, there might be a ray of hope here. I have to try and seize whatever opportunity that may arise.

Some of the volunteers are heading off to Ryan's Steak House in Picayune to eat. They ask me to join them but I have already collected a supper from The Red Cross. I decline, and maybe it is providential because Paul drops by and we spend a long time in deep sharing and discussion. Paul was one of the leaders of our Diocesan SEARCH retreat team when I was Youth Director for the diocese some years ago. We talk about adjustments to be made following the hurricane; some of the struggles and questions in people's minds and how one cannot afford to make quick decisions about the future without standing back and giving it some deep thought and reflection. We talk about his own quandary about coming back to his home town and rebuilding. In fact, prior to the hurricane, he had started building a new home for his family next door to his parents' home. We talk about his children and how they have little roots because they have moved so often due to his navy career. As we chat, I begin to realize the implications of any decision about rebuilding. We also arrange for the baptism of his latest child on Thanksgiving Weekend.

The next morning, the chill in the air awaits me as I arise at my usual early hour. A quick shower and the usual morning chores, along with breakfast and I am on my way to Bay St. Louis. It is now 6:15 a.m. and the traffic does not seem as bad as on previous mornings. As I enter Bay St. Louis, I notice some joggers jogging through the streets. Maybe, this is another sign that some degree of ritual and routine is coming back to people's lives. Later, someone indicates that things are not returning to "normal;" that, instead, there is a new "normality" which is called a "non-normal normality."

Then, it is time for 8:15 a.m. Mass for the children. I use the theme of friendship and question the children about what it was like not to be able to be around their friends after the hurricane or, in many cases, not being able to get in touch with them because they had moved temporarily to another state. I also ask them to think about their friends who have not come back to school with them as yet and to pray for their safe return. The children at school, on the surface, seem happy to be back; but, deep down, I wonder how the trauma of the hurricane and their displaced lives has affected them.

As evening dawns, I decide to go and eat with Dick and Bonnie at the usual feeding place. It is around 6 p.m. and I get a phone call saying that my FEMA trailer has arrived. I believe in miracles. I rush back to see my "Plain Jane" trailer. They are trying to guide it backwards into the slot for it on the slab. Finally, they get it situated and leveled. I do a quick tour and okay it. Then it is time to head home to Diamondhead and my "read Condo." Yes, another milestone is reached. Now, I can join the trailer "haves" and pray for the "have-nots."

The next morning, I receive a phone call from Dorothy in Phoenix. She has a radio show and I will be on live with her. We chat live on the radio for 25 minutes, sharing what the situation is like, some of the frustrations and accomplishments along the way as well as how people can continue to help us. She asks how her audience may be able to help. So, I give her some suggestions. As the end of the interview, she asks me to give a blessing for her audience. I oblige: "May the

Lord bless you and keep you. May the Lord let his face shine upon you and be gracious to you. And give you his peace." I realize the blessing is just as appropriate for me and my community as her audience. The blessing also becomes my prayer and plea for God's blessing.

The Governor's Commission on rebuilding the Coast meet in our Community Center from 3:30—5 p.m. Over five hundred people attend the meeting. The Commission shares ideas on various aspects of rebuilding and asks for input from the floor. The Commission's ideas seem idealistic. Many people show disapproval and hope that the community will not lose its unique character. Some express their anger and frustration at FEMA and their inability to get a trailer. The FEMA representative meets with the people afterwards to answer some of their questions. It promises to be a frustrating experience for the people who have been waiting for answers from FEMA for a long time. At least, now the people waiting for a trailer, can ask some people who, hopefully, have the answers.

Yes, tomorrow arrives sooner than expected and it arrives with a bang. I head down to Bay St. Louis at 6:45 a.m. and the dashboard of the SUV warns me of trouble. I have a flat tire. I ride as far as the gas station by the highway and go to check if there are any repair places in the area. The attendant indicates that there is a place nearby. I walk to check it out only to find that Hurricane Katrina had other plans for it. A gentleman stops by to try and fix it with a flat tire repair but it proves useless. I finally call Jo, our secretary, and have her come to collect me. Maybe, these are not the kind of surprises we like to greet us so early in the morning. Let's hope so! Dick and Bonnie change the flat tire and take it to one of the repair places. The rest of the day is bound to be better.

The sisters of Mrs. Jane come by to talk about their mother and chat about funeral arrangements for their mother who drowned in Hurricane Katrina. They mention that the men in the family stopped going to church years ago because of the way they were treated by nuns in their parish school. Maybe, the funeral on Monday may speak to them and the Lord may use it to touch their hearts and draw them back again to the fold. Let's hope so.

We celebrate Jane's funeral at the local funeral home and then to Biloxi National Cemetery for burial. Brian, one of Jane's sons, attends the funeral, cuddling his little dog. He has his own story of survival; how he and his dog escaped the floodwaters. I realize it must have been a very difficult few weeks for Jane's family. First of all, Jane was drowned during Hurricane Katrina. When the search and rescue team came and found her body, they marked the place and were supposed to come back later that evening but did not. When they finally recovered the body, it was badly decomposed and DMORT really messed things up. They lost the body. They couldn't tell the family anything. The family had to go through weeks of anguish while DMORT tried to sort things out. Finally, they found and released the body for burial today. It is two months later. Now, at least, the family can have closure finally. What an agonizing wait and ordeal!

11

When Will It Be Rebuilt?

I spend some time with some of the reporters, technicians and producers for CNN. They are in the process of producing a one-hour program on the recovery and rebuilding of the Bay St. Louis area.

During the interview, they ask me various questions about Hurricane Katrina; about my own involvement, the disposition of the people, the seemingly overwhelming task that is ahead for everyone.

One of the final questions, Brian, the Producer of the program asks is: "When do you think Bay St. Louis will be rebuilt?" His question is obvious and necessary but the answer is not so obvious or certain, at least, initially.

I answer his question by indicating that one cannot put a deadline or date as to when the city will be rebuilt. I go on to explain that rebuilding is a process not a deadline. It is an ongoing process, not a finished product.

Often we use the old adage, "build it and they will come." People may come to the "field of dreams" but now people's fields of dreams have been shattered. It is easy to dream dreams in the abstract but one wonders if and when people have the ability to rise from the ashes of spent dreams to new ones.

I meet parishioners every day and ask them; "Have you decided what you are going to do?" Most simply answer, "I'm going to wait and see," or "Right now, I really don't know what I am going to do." People are still in shock, traumatized by the destruction and disruption in their life. Now, everything seems so complicated. They feel paralyzed by indecision.

Later, I begin to think more and more about his question as I probe it more deeply.

I discover that rebuilding is a very individual process. Different people have different resources. People react differently to different situations, depending on such resources. Some people are frozen in time, paralyzed by the wrath of the hurricane. Others are paralyzed by their inability to make a decision. Some are in a denial stage, hoping that some day, they will wake up and realize that the hurricane was a mirage. Others decide to run, to run from themselves, and from their trauma. Some decide to hide in the clutches of alcohol. Some even decide to end their lives prematurely. Others discover new energy and resources to rise to the top in determination and resolve.

As a society, we are conditioned to solve problems and issues in a timely manner. We solve a homicide in less than an hour on a TV show. We find all the news that it fit to see and fit to print in less than half-hour.

So often, we try to bring closure to things and events. It is a natural desire but often proves fruitless. Can we ever say we have "made it?" Can we ever indicate that we "know it all?" Can we ever say, we have completed our schooling, completed learning, and completed our growth? I doubt it!

One of the most distasteful kinds of people are people who know it all, who have all the answers, who have nothing to learn, who are experts in everything. They pride themselves in their knowledge, their expertise, their "know it all" mentality that they exude.

As a society, we thrive on deadlines, tasks accomplished, jobs done, status achieved; portfolios enlarged; people impacted, income increased, financial security; expectations met and ladder climbing achievements.

We have our measuring rods, our goals and projections, our comparisons, and our affirmations at having made the grade. We have our barometers to measure our earning power, our true worth, our productivity, our output and our influence amid the movers and shakers.

We are always striving, always trying to reach higher and farther; climb another rung in the ladder of success; improve our portfolio and credibility. We engage in simple makeovers that are just cosmetic and makeovers that are extreme. We are always remodeling our homes, retooling our skills. We engage in continuing education that becomes lifelong learning. We are always experimenting with life's "what ifs" as well as second-guessing our decisions.

We are constantly pruning, grafting and recreating our space, whether it be our little garden or our giant castle. We get bored easily with the mundane, the common, the monotonous and the repetitive. We watch Reality Shows because we are bored with the real which we are constantly changing and manipulating to make it over into our image and likeness.

When someone we love dies, we go through a mourning period. It is filled with emotions, memories, thoughts and experience. Some times, people tell us "it is time to move on." But one cannot put a time limit on "moving on." People deal with grief in different ways, depending on their own resources and support systems.

The same happens when people begin to rebuild their lives, homes and community after a disaster. We are not robots, programmed to react toward certain stimuli. We cannot put a time limit on such. Rebuilding is never finished. One is always growing, always improving, always expanding in more ways.

As I continue to reflect on Brian's question, I journey into my own opportunity to discover how I might begin to rebuild my own life as well as the life of my community.

The Book of Ecclesiastes reminds us, "There is a time for everything," and I discover that time is not always chronological.

12

It Is Thanksgiving Again!

As November rolls around, my thoughts become more reflective. What is this Thanksgiving going to be like? Obviously, it is going to be different. It is not going to be some mythical, feel-good kind of Thanksgiving. It is going to be a much simpler but more profound time. It will be a more reflective time; a time to pause and count real blessings which are not things but relationships.

When I arrive back from my Monday morning duty of traffic cop at our Elementary School, Bill and Carolyn, my special friends from South Dakota, are waiting. I show them around and visit for a while before heading off to Diamondhead for a 10:08 a.m. golf appointment. This is the first time I have been away for a few hours since immediately after Hurricane Katrina. I should prize my sanity a little more.

It is great to get away for a few hours of relaxation and not even bring a cell phone with me. We are joined for golf by Andy and Marcia. Marcia is a very talkative person and takes her golf pretty seriously. I play with borrowed clubs and don't loose too many balls. I even get a few pars, given the fact that my golf game is rusty.

Following golf, I take Bill and Carolyn to show them the condo they will stay in for tonight. Then, we tour some of the devastated areas and they are amazed at the extent of the devastation. We visit some more on their return and then head out for supper to one of the feeding places. We are served chili, beans and mixed vegetables.

When we return home, we visit some more before they head off to Diamondhead for the night. Tonight, I reflect on the value of our friendship and how it has lasted through the years.

The following morning, Dan Quinn arrives. His expertise is computer networking. We discover he also has some tremendous organizational skills which will prove invaluable in the weeks and months ahead. He will be here for a few weeks as he is between jobs. I give him the task of getting our phones and Internet working. Then Eddie stops by to connect our phone lines to the office trailer, and after some difficulties, accomplishes the task. Dan drives to Gulfport to pick up a wireless router so we can share Internet connections at the office.

Within a few days, I perform Tony's funeral. Only a few people attend. I discover that, instead of leaving his home for the hurricane, he locked himself in a room and would not leave. Obviously, he was drowned. I felt sad as I listened to his wife tell me stories of their relationship and the way it ended. He was determined to stay with a sinking ship and both were destroyed. Hopefully, I was able to bring some hope and consolation to his family as they mourned his loss.

Ray calls from the "Irish Echo" in New York to get an update on what has been happening since we last spoke. He did an initial story some weeks ago and has continued to show interest in updating his readers on the ongoing situation I continue to face in rebuilding. He asks for my picture to be put into the next issue. I appreciate his interest and his faithfulness in continuing to keep our story in the news.

Soon, another weekend is upon us as well as an opportunity to meet some new volunteers. Today, volunteers from various parts of Georgia arrive, including about twenty teenagers. Two of our volunteers—a landscaper and his son—are busy sowing rye grass so that we might have green grass eventually. By adding a touch of color to the place will help dampen the drab and bleak landscape. The ladies from Winder, GA. get busy organizing clothes and especially the new shipment from Chicago.

I receive a call from Carolyn informing me that her husband is not doing too well in a hospital in Mandeville. I promise to go and see him tomorrow.

Some leftover soup from lunch suffices for evening meal and a relaxing evening. While relaxing, I get a phone call from Suzanne at "The Wall Street Journal." She is doing a story on the role of statues during the hurricane. I fill her in on some details and give her some persons to call for more information.

The Koch family are busy landscaping and planting flowers, adding a touch of color to our environment. Gerri arrives and it is good to see her. I have not seen her since she graduated from high school. She used to work with us on our Diocesan SEARCH Retreat Team. She joins her mother and Laurie in landscaping.

Lunch includes a Thanksgiving luncheon with the faculty and staff of Bay Catholic Elementary School where we feast on turkey and all the trimmings.

Following lunch, I drive to Mandeville to visit Frank L. in hospital there. While there, I also chat with Carolyn, his wife of 52 years. We chat about his prognosis and she indicates that hospice has been contacted and he would be going to stay at his son's house in the area. While I am there, one of the hospice nurses arrives to pitch her company and answer any questions. An hour later, another hospice person from another company arrives to make another sales pitch for her company. I exit between both presentations; knowing that I will perform another funeral service within a few days.

Today is Thanksgiving Day. As I drive in from Diamondhead, the low-lying fog caresses the ground like a woolen blanket. There is a chill in the air but it is not as bad as previous mornings.

I receive a phone call from Carolyn, letting me know that her husband, Frank, just died. I am glad that I had the opportunity to see him in hospital the other day. Funeral arrangements are set for Monday morning.

This morning, our Mass is at 9 a.m. and quite a crowd gathers to celebrate a simple thanksgiving for being alive, for getting us through the hurricane and for the energy to continue the process of recovery.

Noon arrives and it is time for our Thanksgiving dinner for some families and the volunteers. Through the generosity and courtesy of Terry and Kathleen and their families; we are treated to a wonderful celebration of food and friendship.

The 7 a.m. Mass on the morning after Thanksgiving is less crowded. We understand why. The rest of them must have gone early bird shopping on this "Black Friday."

The next morning, I awake to the pitter patter of rain. It is a welcome sound as I hope it will replenish the dry and scarred earth. As I ride down the highway to Bay St. Louis, the windshield wipers keep a rhythmic cycle as they wipe away the early morning tears of rain. Most of the world along the way is still asleep and the automobile are scarce as we pick out our way down the darkened highway.

I have an hour to get my thoughts together for the day ahead which will begin with Mass at 7:30 a.m. The rain becomes heavier and more persistent as we dodge our way to the Community Center for Mass. Fewer than usual show up, which is understandable because of the weather. Following Mass, the volunteers from Wisconsin present the parish with a generous check from another parish in that area. The generosity of people along the way who have sacrificed to help us in the recovery effort has been a humbling but rewarding experience for us.

We have a baptism at 11 a.m. this morning—Hope Elizabeth. The family and their extended family gather for this celebration as digital and video cameras flicker and shoot their way into history for Hope. Following the baptism, I rush to the funeral home for the service for Irene. She was a resident of Dunbar Village before the hurricane and was evacuated to Meridian. She died in Meridian on September 8th and finally the family are able to bring earthly closure to her life today. They cannot even find her burial place in Waveland so there is no burial for now. Maybe, later.

While at the funeral home, I pick up some sandwiches they have made and take them home for lunch. Obviously, they are leftover turkey.

The early Sunday morning demands our attention as it graces us with its presence. Another day has dawned and wants my attention. I get the usual morning chores out of the way as I head to Bay St. Louis at 6 a.m. The road is quiet and I enjoy a few quiet moments as the PRM radio morning broadcasts some classical music to soothe the spirit.

The 8 a.m. Mass brings out some extra people who remind me that they are now back to stay. This is another milestone in the recovery process.

The 10:30 a.m. Mass brings out even more people than usual. It is exciting to see so many people gathering and scurrying for a chair or a place to stand for our celebration.

It is 1 p.m. and time to head off to Southern Delights restaurant where the family are having a get together meal. I arrive to the welcome by an array of Thanksgiving food which makes the pallet sing with delight. They have the usual turkey and trimmings as well as rich, creamy desserts. I partake and enjoy.

Monday morning, following lunch, I drive to St. Rose Church for Frank's funeral. I am happy that I got an opportunity to have visited him in Mandeville last week before he died. Frank was one of our ushers and greeters at the 8 a.m. Sunday morning Mass. His car was always the first car to arrive for Mass and he and his wife, Carolyn, had their favorite pew in church in the very back row on the side. I was privileged to help them celebrate 50 years of marriage two years ago.

As the month of November gradually disappears into the history books, I sit down to reflect on this month of Thanksgiving.

So what am I thankful for this Thanksgiving?

I am thankful for being alive; for discovering that the Lord still has a plan that is unfolding for me.

I am thankful for realizing my own weakness which has made me more reliant on the power and strength of God working in and through me.

I am thankful for the thousands of volunteers—many whose names we will never know—who came to our rescue; who mucked out our homes; cleaned out our debris; fed us our meals and watched out for our safety.

I am thankful for the reporters who came, not just looking for a quick sound-bite, but who were genuinely interested in our story and sharing it and our recovery with the world.

I am thankful for reporters like Kathleen who is not afraid to show how a story is more than a story especially when it touches one personally.

I am thankful for people like the two "Dan's"—Wilkens and Quinn—who left family, job and security of home to come and coordinate our volunteer efforts.

I am thankful for the hundreds of people who sacrificed wages and savings to help us financially in the rebuilding process.

I am thankful for the support staff—to Jo, Kathleen, and Mary—who continue to journey with us in the recovery process.

I am thankful for people like Janice and Jackie who work tireless behind the scenes, without looking for recognition, to make sure our children and young people can enjoy school again.

I am thankful for builders like Mike who takes on, as his own ministry, the task of rebuilding our devastated church.

I am thankful for the spectacular morning sunrises, courtesy of God, which remind me that today is a new day that is filled with hope and promise.

I am thankful for friends like Mike and Mary Ann and their family for their hospitality; their air mattress and their friendship.

I am thankful for friends like Chuck who, unselfishly, provides me with more clothes to put on my back, other than the ones I arrived back from vacation with.

I am thankful for the many people who genuinely ask, "Is there anything we can do for you?" or "Is there anything you need?" and are willing to put it into action.

I am thankful for the wisdom I have learned over the years as it continues to help me make the important and timely decisions that need to be made.

I am thankful for the gift of faith, even though often questioned, yet, never prone to despair.

I am thankful that, I may be able to bring some hope to people who have lost loved ones during or since the hurricane.

I am thankful that, even thought it seems overwhelming at best, I have been given the ministry of rebuilding, not only parish facilities but, more especially, giving hope to people who may have lost everything.

I am thankful for my real family, who constantly call with their support, prayers and encouragement.

I am thankful for the countless young people who came to us from high schools and colleges to contribute to the rebuilding process because it gives me hope for the future leadership.

I am thankful for people like the Koch family, who gave up their Thanksgiving holidays to celebrate a working reunion landscaping in our community.

I am thankful for people like Steve who set up our special Katrina web site for us, allowing us to communicate our story, both in print and visually, with the outside world.

I am thankful for my digital camera that has faithfully captured our dying and rising as a community.

I am thankful for friends like Bill and Carolyn who keep in touch constantly, visit and support us in our recovery effort.

I am thankful for long-time friends John and Terry and their family for their ongoing efforts to elicit support from their community.

I am thankful for the couple from Illinois who offered me their condominium to stay in and enjoy some time away from the rubble, debris and wanton destruction.

I am thankful for the many lessons I continue to learn and discover as I journey through the aftermath of the hurricane.

I am thankful for the little things I had taken for granted because of my busyness and rushing around in the past but, now I treasure them even more.

I am thankful for the people who drop by and simply ask, "How are you doing? Are you okay?" and who genuinely want to know the truth.

I am thankful for the hugs I have received as people affirm me in my goodness and that I am doing a good job.

I am thankful for office breaks where we can sit around over a cup of coffee or tea and share the impact of Katrina on our life, our family and our spirits.

I am thankful for the letters that arrive daily reminding me that someone—stranger or friend—are proud of me and are praying for me.

I am thankful for the simple sounds that my busyness didn't allow me to hear, especially the sound of silence.

I am thankful for the gift of patience; many times tried; always honed and always needed.

I am thankful for an attitude to life that is part genes, part upbringing, part pruned and always ready to do battle with whatever forces it meets.

I am thankful for quiet evenings without the din of TV which allows my soul to drink in the distilled and nourishing waters of prayer and reflection.

I am thankful for less clutter in my life so I can make more room in my heart for more soul food.

13

It's Just a Simple Christmas

It is December again and my thoughts turn toward Christmas. The thoughts are complicated but, while I realize that Christmas is a simple feast; it also creates a profound effect on us.

As I carry all kinds of conflicting thoughts around in my head, a gentleman comes by to check on the church. He stops me and says that he was here some months ago after the hurricane. He mentions that he went into the church then and cried when he saw it. He says, "We hope you are saving the old lady." I assured him that we are.

On December 8th there is the usual early morning—3 a.m., wake up. When I finally get up just before 5 a.m., I hear the cell phone go off as I am in the shower. A million thoughts go through my mind, wondering who might be calling me that early in the morning. I check the phone and I get an "unavailable" for the phone number. I wonder if it is from Ireland. One often thinks of the worst and wonders. Is there something wrong? Has someone died? Could it be an emergency? I hang around to see if someone might call again, but they don't so I give up, realizing that if the phone call was important, they would call back again. I finally leave at 5:40 a.m. and arrive in Bay St. Louis at around 6 a.m.

The Christmas tree arrives for the front lawn of our church. It is courtesy of Scott Bridge—the ones who are building the railroad bridge nearby. This is the first tangible signs of Christmas. Inside, I try to be excited, but there is still hollowness within.

I discover that the "Search and Rescue Team" who recovered the bodies of Ralph and Johanna, are ready to hand them over to the family. Some days later, I perform their funeral services at the local funeral home. A large crowd gathers to support the family—especially the three daughters. I visit with them beforehand and they share with me how the eldest daughter and her husband had stayed with their parents in the house during the hurricane. The daughter and her husband clung to a tree while they watched her parents being washed away. The ordeal must have been very traumatizing for them. The husband indicates that the Lord must have spared them for a reason. One of the daughters and a family friend shares some moving thoughts about the deceased. Later on, some parishioners recount how they rescued the daughter and son-in-law but were unable to grab onto their parents. I wonder what it is like to see your parents being carried away in the flood waters and realize that this will be your last glimpse of them. The memory will probably be etched deep in their psyches. It will be a tough Christmas for the remaining family.

It is already the Tuesday before Christmas, The bishop is supposed to arrive today to visit with students at Our Lady Academy. I get a phone call from the Principal to inform me. He is supposed to bring a bishop and some other personnel from Wisconsin with him.

Following the lunch, I notice that the entourage passes by my office window and heads into church to view the destruction. Maybe, they will drop by and check on me and ask how I am doing, how things are going with the recovery. But, it is all wishful thinking. They get into the car and head off. To put it mildly, I am disappointed. I could use stronger words but they will remain unwritten for now. I will let the action speak for itself.

This evening at 6:30 p.m., we join the children at Bay Catholic Elementary for their Christmas program. The place is crammed with parents, grandparents and children packed like sardines in the Community Center. There is no need for heat as body heat takes care of the cold evening chill. Parents armed with their latest video and digital cameras snap their little ones in their debut. It is a beautiful spectacle, especially when people have lost so much.

I leave there to attend a Parish Planning Meeting at Richard's house. Most of the folks are gathered there and the food is good and plentiful. I don't have to worry about supper this evening and even indulge with seconds.

Then, there is a surprise. I discover that the gathering is not so much for a meeting but to present me with a gift. I open the first gift and discover a package of golf tees and a box of golf balls. Then they bring in a golf bag and a long box which I open to discover a full set of Wilson golf clubs. It is ironic that before the meeting I was checking the Internet to see if there were any good deals on golf clubs. I am in awe over the beautiful surprise, the generosity and thoughtfulness of the group. Momentarily, I compare it with my disappointment with the entourage earlier in the day that passed me by. Now, I discover the real care and love of people and that makes it all worthwhile. This "surprise" will help make Christmas simple, but rewarding.

With a spring in my step, in spite of the night chill, I head off to Diamondhead to bring the day to a close. At 9 p.m. I tumble in under the sheets and quickly fall asleep.

The day before Christmas Eve arrives. I awake to thoughts, reflections and efforts to put a hurricane in perspective at 2 a.m. in the morning. Memories, incidents, snippets of conversations, stories and experiences flood my mind. My mind races ahead as I try to put some perspective on what flows so freely. The thoughts and ideas bombard me. If only I had my laptop nearby, I might be able to capture some of them as raw material for my book experience on the hurricane.

Breakfast is rather sparse—a glass of orange juice. I forgot to get some cereal last night. Breakfast will have to wait until I get to the office. I leave the apartment at 5:35 a.m. and head to Bay St. Louis. First, I have to negotiate the frosted windshield as I give it a blast of hot air from inside. Gradually, it does the trick and I head down the road.

It is still dark when I arrive. A cup of tea and a roll makes up for a postponed breakfast. I munch and drink while I check news, emails and respond. By then, it is time for 7 a.m. Mass. As we begin Mass, a glorious sunrise gradually lifts its head over the horizon. Someone mentioned that we are going to miss the sunrises when we move into the church. Hopefully, we will continue to recognize his presences in the gifts of every new day.

I am finally able to capture my thoughts and write them down. They flow freely without editing as I try to capture what I envision as my "Simple Christmas."

The reporter with Catholic News Service asked me, "How are you going to celebrate Christmas this year?" My answer was a direct one—"just a simple Christmas." I went on to explain.

This year, I will celebrate a simple Christmas because there is very little clutter in my life right now. Hurricane Katrina divested me of all my personal belonging and now I don't have to worry about accumulating or divesting. She was a great teacher.

This year, I will celebrate a simple Christmas without the distractions, without knee-jerk reactions to sales pitches or bargains. They have been dethroned to their rightful place.

This year, I will celebrate a simple Christmas in the company of my parishioners and friends who will share the common bond of simplicity with me.

This year, I will celebrate a simple Christmas because in my emptiness, I can be filled with a much richer and lasting Gift.

This year, I will celebrate a simple Christmas without fanfare or frivolity that might become escape hatches through which I dare not go anymore.

This year, I will celebrate a simple Christmas with simplicity of faith that draws me even deeper into the Mystery of the season.

This year, I will celebrate a simple Christmas with a spirit of gratitude for what I have gained rather than what I lost; for what I have discovered about others than what I ignored; for what I have discovered about myself than what was obvious for so long.

This year, I will celebrate a simple Christmas, realizing that "it's a wonderful life" is real and not just the title of a movie.

This year, I will celebrate a simple Christmas, knowing that I will continue to discover a new birth within myself that will astonish and captivate me.

This year, I will celebrate a simple Christmas because I am reminded that it was the simple people with uncluttered lives that recognized and celebrated that first Christmas.

This year, I will celebrate a simple Christmas by being homeless, knowing that new birth can and will take place in our places of displacement.

This year, I will celebrate a simple Christmas because God has got my attention and when he has, He is always ready to be born anew within me.

This year, I will celebrate a simple Christmas by being and becoming what God wanted me to become and not doing so that I might receive the recognition of others.

This year, I will celebrate a simple Christmas by being more at home with my own journey rather than being guided by the fleeting signposts that seem to surround me.

This year, I will celebrate a simple Christmas by reflecting on the gift of personhood rather than the gift-wrapped.

This year, I will celebrate a simple Christmas by filling my heart with an expectation that can only be filled with the gift of a Person.

This year, I will celebrate a simple Christmas because its miracle will take place within me, not on 34th Street.

This year, I will celebrate a simple Christmas because there is a child within me yearning to be born just like the Christ Child who changed the world.

This year, I will celebrate a simple Christmas by allowing its quiet to permeate my life.

This year, I will celebrate a simple Christmas by continuing to embark on a journey of discovery while I am led by the hand of God.

This year, I will celebrate a simple Christmas in the quiet spaces of my life which yield a clearer map for life's journey.

This year, I will celebrate a simple Christmas by taking census of my blessings, instead of my crosses; my gifts instead of my wants and my emptiness instead of my satisfaction.

This year, I will celebrate a simple Christmas because the mystery and message of Christmas is profoundly simple.

Last Sunday, I left parishioners with the message; "We will see you in Church for Christmas!" Many clap in jubilations; others, more practical, wonder if it is possible. They have to wait and see if another miracle of Christmas takes place for them.

It is Christmas Day. It is a day to celebrate, celebrate even our simplicity, our loss, our hopes and yes, our recovery. We will gather to remember again the birth of a Child who came to lead us and our world on a journey of recovery centuries ago. He still comes, even at the darkest hours of Katrina.

It is 5:40 a.m. as I pull the door of the apartment closed and check to make sure it is locked. My car jumps to attention and is ready to take me to a sacred place where we will celebrate birth and rebirth.

The highway is deserted. National Public Radio beams out "The Halleluiah Chorus" from Handel's Messiah. As I listen to its vibrations, I try to invite it deep into my spirit. As I drive along to its strains, the vestiges of Hurricane Katrina still catch my attention. I notice that crumbled trailer still hugging the side of the road. Fresh debris, cleaned out from recently returning residents stand awkwardly near the roadway. People have emptied out their homes and maybe their hearts and souls as they pray for a fresh start. Maybe, they will find it in the hope that Christmas is waiting to offer them.

It is quiet here as I sit at my computer. Gently but consistently, the sun is rising to the occasion. An orange glow encompasses the waiting day. The clear blue sky reminds us it is time to celebrate the birth of a royal king.

Soon, it is time for our Christmas Day Masses. I have pondered long and hard what message of hope I might share with the people this Christmas. Obviously, it has to be a message of hope, seeing that they have experienced one of the deadliest and darkest times in their lives. The words begin to flow like an unstoppable faucet. I try to capture them.

"I am very confused this Christmas. The song that keeps coming to mind isn't any of the Christian Christmas songs, like "Away in a Manger," "Silent Night" or "Angels we have heard on High." The song that keeps coming to my mind is "I'll be home for Christmas." I wonder why. I know it is a song, recorded by many artists, most notably Bing Crosby. The song touches the hearts of both soldier and civilians at the time during World War II. Obviously, it reflects the wish of a soldier to be home for Christmas especially, the last two lines are the most haunting, "I'll be home for Christmas; if only in my dreams."

We are home for Christmas and it is not just a dream. I told you we would see you in Church this Christmas. It is no longer a dream; it is a reality. Yes, we are home for Christmas; home where we celebrate every Christmas; home where we celebrate our baptisms, First Confessions, First Communions, Confirmations, Weddings and family funerals. This is our home. This is our faith family home and we gather to celebrate another homecoming; the coming of the Christ-Child into the home of our hearts.

Yes, we are at home in our parish church for Christmas. Look around you. A lot has happened since we last celebrated Mass here on August 28th. Look around you. The floor is bare. The pews are gone. The paint is peeling again. The altar rails are no more. The two angels that guarded our entrance are battered and beaten. Our stained glass windows are shattered. Our carpet is history. Our holy water fonts are non-existent. Our air conditioning and heating is destroyed. Our refurbished organ is silenced. Our doors are blown out. The dampness has turned black. But, we are here and we're home for Christmas and it is not a dream.

Maybe, just maybe, we are like this threadbare church that we stand in. Of course, we are. A lot has happened to us since August 29th. We have become threadbare also. Our homes are gone. Our belongings are history. Our family heirlooms are washed away. Our jobs have been derailed. Our comforts have turned into discomforts. Our normality has turned into a more uncertain non-normality. Our vehicles rose and sank with the rising waters. Our mud infected property became a treacherous nightmare. Our FEMA trailers are not meant for more than one person. Our grocery shopping escapades leaves us with few choices. Our eating habits are irregular. Our minds play tricks on us. Our bodies are weary with worry and stress. Our future plans are non-existent or at best uncertain. Our community is in shambles. Our friends and neighbors are scattered around the country. Our faith is tested with doubt and we wonder where we will get the strength to carry on. We don't know what to believe anymore.

It all sounds depressing, devastating, and hopeless. But there is hope and it is here among the charred surroundings of this church. This church stands as a testament to her age and her wisdom. She has weathered many storms and hurricanes—1947, Camille and now, Katrina. They threw at her all their might, fury and anger but she still stands strong and proud, even if she is a little crushed.

Yes, we are home for Christmas and it is not a dream. It is real. This is our home; the home of our faith where we were baptized made our First Confession, Communion, Confirmation, Wedding and even buried our loved ones from here. We keep coming back to it. Why? Because this is the anchor of our faith. This is where we come to pray, to ask, to celebrate, to receive advice, nourishment and strength. We looked into this place every weekend since August 29th and wondered when if ever we would gather here again. Our wondering is over. We have come home; home to our place of worship; home to each other and home to our God.

Yes, we come with heavy hearts; with more questions than answers; with fears and doubts but open to possibilities.

We come to hear about the birth of a child who came into our world at the bleakest and most desolate time; a child who eventually was to grow up and redeem us. We come to that same Christ Child to redeem us from the hell of Katrina. We celebrate that Christ Child, Emmanuel—God is with us.

Christmas is God's way of reminding us that when life is at its darkest and people are filled with doubt and despair, he comes to remind us—God is with us. Yes, in spite of everything, we have reason to celebrate. We are alive for a reason. Our work is still unfinished and God is with us to bring it to completion. As John's gospel reminds us, 'the light shines on in the darkness and the darkness cannot overcome it;' even the darkness of Hurricane Katrina. Yes, the Word was made flesh and dwells among us.

So, this Christmas, maybe now I know why "I'll be Home for Christmas" kept coming to mind. Maybe it is because, not only are we at home in our church, but God has made his home among us. Even God says, "I'll be home for Christmas and it will be for real."

14

Restless Days and Restless Nights

I indicated earlier in this book, that the church sign at Our Lady of the Gulf Church in Bay St. Louis, Mississippi, read; "It is when you loose everything that you are free to do anything." That particular saying continues to haunt me in the aftermath of Hurricane Katrina. I remember before going on vacation, giving some quotes to our maintenance person to put on our Church sign. It seems providential that the above quote greeted people prior to the hurricane. Obviously, Katrina took care of making sure we lost the sign as well.

I continue to wrestle with the saying that graced that sign. Is it accidental? Providential? or just the bearer of a hidden message? Others wonder the same. I continue to muse over it during some of my restless days and restless nights.

Yes, I have lost everything; so, am I free to do anything? What does that "anything" really mean? Does it mean that I have to lose everything in order to be free? Does it mean that I have to give up control in order to be really free to do anything? Does it mean that I have to give up my comfort zones in order to be really free to embrace the unknown? Why do I have to loose everything? Could it not be loosing a little and gaining a little? My mind begins to play tricks with me as I try to decipher its metaphorical handwriting on the wall?

As I reflect on my journey through the aftermath of Hurricane Katrina and its opportunity for loss, pain and possible growth; I realize the growing pains continue.

I find myself wearing two hats through all the growing pains of Katrina. First of all, I am a human being who has lost everything. Because of that, I am experiencing my own psychological wounds. I feel like, Damian of Molokai who spent his life working with the lepers in Hawaii. When he contracted leprosy himself, he was able to address the lepers as "fellow lepers."

Secondly, I wear the hat of bring a priest, a counselor. Wearing that hat, indicates that I am cast into the role of a caregiver, a psychologist, a counselor; as one who provides assistance and emotional support for fellow journeyers who experience losing everything and/or are trying to move through the stages of their own grief to healing. At times, it seems like one is a split-personality.

The turmoil increases when I try to reconcile what seems like opposites; that is being both the person needing healing and being the person who helps people experience healing. Then, again, I ask myself: am I supposed to reconcile both? Am I not really expected to understand that even opposites can attract and even be compatible? To my curious mind, I find, what seems like a contradiction, really to be a challenge. I journey along, embracing the challenge; open to discover its lessons. I also hope to discover something about myself; my own resilience; my own faith; my own gifts; and my own ability to grow creatively as a person.

I may now be beginning to understand what spiritual writer, Henri Nouwen, wrote when he said we are all "wounded healers."

First of all, I need to ponder how, I, as an individual, journey through my own grieving process to eventual healing. Secondly, once I try to understand my own journey through grief to healing; then, I will be able to help others.

So, how do I make the journey through loosing "everything" to the healing realization that I am "free to do anything"?

First of all, I realize that, while I am on vacation, I first hear of the possible threat of a hurricane. I am not worried initially because the hurricane is going to hit "some place else," not really in my town. The worse scenario, as I look at it from afar, is that; if it does strike close to our area, my home will survive because it was built following Hurricane Camille in 1969 and it was built "hurricane proof." So, I don't need to be overly worried. Even when I discover that my area receives a direct hit, I am shaken and distraught but not completely devastated. When Kathleen, our Pastoral Associate, calls me and informs me that "the rectory is gone" and goes on to tell me that my "car is gone," I ask her, "Who moved it (my car)?" I am still in denial. It cannot be that bad. Even when friends email me an aerial picture of the area; I am still in denial as I can still see familiar landmarks so it still cannot be that bad.

Once it begins to sink in that the devastation is catastrophic, I begin to go into hibernation. I need to be left alone. I need space and time to try and sort out what I will have to come to terms with. Immediately, I go for a long walk along a deserted country road. I know I will not meet anyone along that road. I do not want to engage in conversation with anyone. I know that, in the time ahead, there will be periods when I might want to wake up and realize that this is just a bad dream or that I will still need some quiet time when I shield myself from others so I can continue to process my own feelings.

As I continue on this stage, I discover others there, too. I discover others saying, "One day, I am going to wake up and discover that this was just a horrible nightmare."

Secondly, I find myself angry. I am angry that I have to return to devastation rather than business as usual. I am angry because I have to start all over again. I go back from vacation with the clothes on my back. I go back to disaster, devastation, catastrophe and uncertainty. I go back to the realization that I have lost everything. It is not fair! What about all the professional and personal books, DVD's, CD's, Videos that I had accumulated during the past thirty-three years? What about my computer system; even all the backup's I had made as well as the original program disks? Then there is all that research I just finished on upcoming workshops I am slated to give. I am angry that I have to start all over there again? I also had a collection of my weekly homilies during the last several years and they are gone too and that makes me angry. I also had backed up all the articles I had written for newspapers since I started writing back in 1973. Now, they, too, are gone, and I am angry.

I am angry too, because all the remodeling and upgrading we did on our church during the past few years, have been wrested from our heart and the hearts of the people who spearheaded the efforts and the people who enjoyed their fruits until a cruel Katrina decided to pillage her.

As I listen to other's anger, I realize they are feeling the same kinds of anger. All their memories, possessions, homes, jobs are non-existent. Their dreams; comfort zones; security are filled with the mud and debris left by Katrina. Their hopes for their children; their life's savings; their plans for college are all derailed.

This anger is directed at various sources. They are angry at God, as they ask, "God, why me?" "What did I do wrong?" "Why would you destroy us, especially that we are church-going; God-fearing people?"

The anger is also directed at all branches of the government, whether justified or not. "Mr. President, do you really care?" "Why did you not send help sooner?" "Why did I not get my FEMA trailer?" "Why is New Orleans getting all the publicity and no one cares about us on the Mississippi Gulf Coast?"

Neighbors who came through the hurricane unscathed are also the victims of other people's anger. "Why did they get off so lucky" "Why did my house get destroyed and they didn't even loose a few shingles from their roof?"

Of course, insurance companies get their own share of the anger. As one old lady says, "I have been paying my insurance for years; giving and giving and giving because they told me I was in good hands; now when it is their turn to give back, they don't even know you. They disappear."

Thirdly, I find myself trying to make bargains, especially with God. "Okay! God, if you help me find…I promise I will be a more prayerful and committed person." I test my bargaining power but the results are slim. I search through the rubble and debris in the hopes of finding something significant from my past that would connect me through the present to the future. The search proves futile and the anger doesn't seem to abate.

I notice the same bargaining attitude in others. Some come and say, "I know this must be a wake up call from God. He sure got my attention. I haven't been much of a churchgoer the last few years but if he gets me through this, then I will try to be a better person." Others chant the familiar phrase; "If only I could…." There is a slim hope built in with a tinge of reality.

As I move beyond the bargaining stage, I discover a fourth stage on my journey which leads to depression. I sit and stew in the ashes of my home, my possessions, my memories, my comfort zones and feel paralyzed. I don't want to be around anyone. I don't want to see anyone. I don't want anyone to come near me. I just want to be left alone. I don't want to listen to or to have to deal with anyone else's depressing story. I have my own depressing story and that is more than enough for me to handle right now. I just want my space. I am angry. I am depressed and don't try to tell me, "it is time to move one" or "you need to get over it," or "you need to snap out of it." This is me right now and you have to accept me where I am right now. Don't try to change me. Don't try to tell me things will get better. Maybe, they will, but, right now, I am simply too depressed to think about anything else.

Sometimes, I walk around, trying to be busy; trying to be preoccupied with something. I hope that such busyness will distract me from the inner turmoil and soul-piercing pain I feel deep inside. Maybe, by being busy, I will not have time to think about the unpleasant, the future climb out of the mire and dirt. But, somehow, in spite of such busyness, during quiet moments, the depressing shock sends me deeper into my inner vulnerability and fragility.

I find others experiencing the same thing. They are paralyzed. They look at the destruction. They do not know where to start. They do not know if they want to start. They just want to walk away and hope it will go away. They are too old. They don't have the energy anymore to start all over again. What is the point? You rebuild and then along comes another hurricane. I also know some who, because of that depression, decided to end it all with a single gunshot or an overdose.

As I continue my journey, hopefully, I come to a fifth and final stage on that journey of recovery. I begin to accept. I realize I cannot change the fact of the hurricane. I cannot bring back my former home; my possessions—both personal and professional. I cannot salvage my car that I hoped would see me through until retirement. I cannot find anything worth keeping amid the ruins and debris of my former home. I am beginning to come to terms with what has happened. I am realizing that I must play the hand of cards that have been dealt me; even though I might have wished otherwise.

Even though I may resent it terribly, I accept the fact that I have to start all over again. I know that, as I do, there will be other painful discoveries and growing pains along the way. There will be questions about my own capabilities; my own inner strength; my own ability to not only rebuild our parish facilities, but more importantly, our parish family and community.

Yes, I may wish things were otherwise; that I didn't have to lie in this bed of pain; work in this rot; face this uncertainty daily. But, I have no choice but to embrace it, live with it and work through it.

As I reflect on the elements of this journey of recovery, I realize that what takes me through one stage to the next is the gift of hope. I realize that I dialogue with myself through writing and diary keeping; that hope is the eternal spark that keeps my fire of perseverance burning.

What am I discovering about myself in this journey of recovery? I am discovering that there are at least three necessary ingredients involved in the recovery process. I call it "The Three T's"—Talk. Tears and Time. In fact, I use this process in my ministry as I try to lead people through disasters they experience—big or small. This process is simple, commonsensical and necessary.

First of all, I need to talk about the Katrina experience. This is an obvious fact. How do I talk about? I talk about it through a gift I have honed over the years—the gift of writing. By talking about it—putting it on paper, I am giving myself permission to let it out; give it some fresh air; allow it to sit there; read over it; see if any of it makes sense and if it has any shape or form that will help me. I know that if I don't find an outlet for it, it will fester like a cancer within me and poison the rest of my life. I know that if I don't talk about/write about it; it will not go away. I need to talk about it/write about it in order to be able to understand it eventually.

Recently, my good friend, Terry, asked me, "Do you ever get tired talking about it?" Sometimes, I have no choice but to talk about it especially when people ask about the hurricane, how I am doing, or how much progress we are making. Other times, I want to move beyond the talking stage so that I don't get stuck, like an old gramophone needle, on the same track.

Secondly, I need to be able to shed some tears if I am to recover fully from Katrina. I know this has nothing to do with being manly or being a sign of weakness. I know it is a very human form of expression as well as a necessary one. I don't have to apologize for my tears. They are real. They are "me." And I have to realize tears are the most natural part of being human. After all, there are tears of sorrow and tears of joy and they are both necessary ingredients to being human. My tears become therapeutic vehicles to healing and wholeness.

Finally, I need time; my own time; not time set by a clock but time determined by my own inner resources; a time that is not chronological or governed by clock-watching. I know that everyone deals with things differently. No one can impose on me their timetable nor can I do the same to them. No one can say to me, "It is time to move on." Only I will know when that time arrives. No one can say, "You should be over that by now." Only I will know for sure when I have worked through it completely.

As I engage in my own "Three T's," I realize that I can move from anger to acceptance; from open wounds to healing balm; from pain to growth; from status quo to challenge and from brokenness to wholeness. I know that as I move through the many transitions; others have to do the same; many of them, with the insights, wisdom and strength I gain from the broken places in my own life.

In order to continue that movement, I need to make various choices along the way. I know that, everything is a choice, according to Matthew Kelly, in his best-selling book, "The Rhythm of Life—Living Every Day with Passion & Purpose;" "It is life's greatest truth and its hardest to learn. It is a great truth because it reminds us of our power. Not power over others, but the often untapped power to be ourselves and to live the life we have imagined.

It is a hard lesson because it causes us to realize that we have chosen the life we are living now. It is perhaps frightening for us to think that we have chosen to live our life exactly as it is today; frightening because we may not like what we find when we look at our lives today. But it is also liberating because we can now begin to choose what we will find when we look at our life in the tomorrows that lie unlived before us."

We did not choose Hurricane Katrina, but we did choose to live in an area that is prone to hurricanes. When we choose, we also choose the implications as well as the challenges we may face as a result of such a choice.

15

Inconclusive Conclusions

When I was assigned to Our Lady of the Gulf parish in Bay St. Louis, Mississippi on September 20, 2000, little did I know what might lie ahead.

A friend, Gina, who has the gift of discernment, shared two prophecies regarding my future. Firstly, I was to write a "Parish Prayer" for my new parish. Secondly, I would be "stretched" in my new parish. She had visions of me walking on millions and millions of sand grains.

I now understand the metaphor of walking on the sand. Obviously, our property was covered with tons of sand, blown in from the beach by Hurricane Katrina. Our property became an array of sand dunes.

It is only now that I am beginning to know the wisdom of such prophecies and their implications.

First of all, our "Parish Prayer" continues to touch the hearts of hundreds of people who recite it daily. Many indicate that the prayer is more timely now in the context of Hurricane Katrina.

The prayer is as follows:

> Lord God, we come to you.
> We come with our hopes and our dreams,
> our fears and our failures,
> our faith and our doubts,
> our troubles and our triumphs.
> We ask you to walk with us
> throughout our days,
> giving us faith when we waver,
> hope when we despair,
> love when we need it most,
> Heal us in our brokenness,
> love us in our shortcomings,
> encourage us in our misgivings,

> empower us with your Spirit.
> Renew us in your life, love and peace
> so we can renew others through
> Christ, Our Lord. Amen.

Secondly, now I am beginning to understand what it means to be "stretched," as Gina reminded me through the gift of discernment. Initially, I was scared; scared of the implications of being "stretched." I wondered what it really meant. I asked myself all kinds of questions: How will I be stretched? Will I know when it is happening? Will I have the resources needed? Will there be a breaking point? And if there is, will I stretch without breaking? Do I have any choice? Can I say "No" to this stretching? Will I discover things about myself in the process that I may not like or have difficulty accepting? What if I break in the process? Will I have the support network to put my "Humpty Dumpty" brokenness back together again? Yes, I am being "stretched" in ways I never dreamed of or imagined. I am beginning to ask myself, "What is Katrina teaching me?"

Katrina is teaching me never to take anything or anyone for granted because some day, that "anything" or "anyone" might be wrenched from my inner being.

Katrina is teaching me to value friendships more than things because things can be replaced and friendships which are taken for granted may not.

Katrina is teaching me that I am never in complete control of life; that I have no choice but to live it as a mystery, not a problem to be solved.

Katrina is teaching me more about myself, a self that is constantly in process, a self that is always in transition.

Katrina is teaching me that perspective is determined by my willingness to grow through adversity.

Katrina is teaching me about the inherent goodness of people who unselfishly and without the need for recognition shine at the darkest hour.

Katrina is teaching me that just as it is darkest just before dawn; that our greatest potential surfaces in seemingly hopeless situations.

Katrina is teaching me that hope, coupled with faith and a generous supply of love, can move us even through the worst disaster.

Katrina is teaching me more about myself than any book could ever as I become an open script for the book of life that the Author of life is writing through me.

Katrina is teaching me I can never really know myself fully until I am stretched on an ongoing basis.

Katrina is teaching me that if I use the raw materials that the Lord has blessed me with, then he will provide me with the blueprints that will guide me on life's journey.

Katrina is teaching me to love surprises, as big as a hurricane or as small as a morning greeting.

Katrina is teaching me that the Lord, who knows me most intimately, believes in me enough to take me through the darkest moments to new life, new growth and new possibilities.

Katrina is teaching me that weakness is a special gift because it allows me to lean more on the Great Architect of my life.

Katrina is teaching me that tears are a gift which can cleanse not only the eye but also the insight which comes from deep within.

Katrina is teaching me that a few minutes of fame may be fleeting, but can become a stimulant to impact lives behind the scenes.

Katrina is teaching me that it is okay to accept a compliment if I am willing to use it as an extra incentive.

Katrina is teaching me that time is not necessarily chronological but instead is programmed by my own gifts, opportunities, courage and determination.

Katrina is teaching me that life is cyclical; that everything has its seasons; that there is a time for everything under the heaven and under the deep recesses of my heart.

Katrina is teaching me that life is a journey that is sometimes disrupted by a pebble in a shoe or a hurricane in a Gulf Coast bottleneck.

Katrina is teaching me that interruptions are really opportunities, some times in sheep's clothing and other times, in wolves clothing.

Katrina is teaching me that often the most scenic as well as the most difficult part of the journey's terrain is the richest and most life-giving as well as life-changing.

Katrina is teaching me that I will never be able or should I be able to put a period where in fact there is simply a pause.

16

Healing Postscripts

Hurricane Katrina spins stories that have a greater force than its 125 m.p.h. winds. These are stories of tears and triumphs; catastrophe and courage; bewilderment and bravery; resignation and recovery; helplessness and hopefulness; despair and determination; envy and endurance; powerlessness and possibility; the ordinary and the extraordinary; the human spirit and the spark of the divine.

Everyone has a story to share because of her; a wisdom to build on; an experience to pass on to generations yet unborn. This story unfolds in the day to day happenings in people's lives. They are as spectacular as an early morning sunrise or as frightening as a militant sea.

Anna Sharp is a Junior at Our Lady Academy High School in Bay St. Louis. Her family had eight feet of water in their home and has to rebuild their lives and homes from the stubborn studs which will again support a home. Anna writes:

You never realize…

You never realize what you have until it's gone. do you know how many times that has played in my head?
I used to take so many things for granted.
Now, I find myself hanging onto every moment of time.
I used to worry about everything.
Now I find myself without a worry in the world.
I used to rely on tomorrow.
Now I find that there may never be a tomorrow.

I saw my life as if it were just another material possession.
But you can't buy life. You only get one.
You only get one chance to live.
You have to live in the moment.
Live like there's no tomorrow.

People say that they don't know what they'd do if they lost everything.
Well, all I can say about that is that it's not that great, but it's not completely horrible either.
With losing everything, I've learned to accept things that I've never accepted before.
I've accepted change…something I never thought I would ever accept.
I've accepted death…the trees and wildlife are dead, and my house and memories are gone.
I've accepted life…I'm closer than ever before with my friends.
I've accepted loss…I've lost people that were extremely close to me, they've moved to other states and have new, better lives.
I've accepted it all.
You may think that nothing good will come out of this, but trust me, there is, and it's happening as we speak.

We've lost everything but it's NOT the end of the world. Be happy you're alive…see this as a chance to start over. Maybe there's a chance now to rekindle old friendships. Or maybe you've always wanted a better wardrobe…well, here's your chance. I know you never pictured yourself in a million years going to a tent every night and picking up free meals, instead of going to that favorite restaurant of yours. And now you find yourself digging through cardboard boxes, filled with clothes and simple necessities, which you NEVER imagined before. And you're accepting things from people who you've never met before, and there's no way to pay them back, you're just so thankful for their graciousness.

And you never thought in a million years, that after a hurricane, something that happens to us six months out of every year, would take away everything you've ever had. And I know you think about it every day.

There are moments when I'm on my way home and for a second I am convinced that I'll be walking through my front door, kicking my shoes off in the corner of the living room and heading straight for the computer to go talk to my friends.

There are times when I'm driving down the road and for a moment it feels like it was before…a feeling that you would do anything for to feel once again. A feeling of security, a feeling that nothing can be taken away from me and everything is fine.

There are places I go, and I remember great times that I've shared with friends and family. Almost everywhere I go reminds me of something. And I know it does the same for you.

Don't run from this…learn from this…

If you run, you're denying…
If you stay, you're accepting…

Yesterday is gone…but we still have the memories…

Anna Sharp, December 5, 2005

Anna's mother, Jo, continues to journey through her own cross to resurrected hope. Her Christmas reflection captures part of that journey.

Dear Father Tracey,

This evening, after I got home from work, I asked Anna to help me move the Crab Fest picnic table you let us borrow into our house so that I would have a gift wrapping table. By doing so I was afforded sufficient room to wrap presents and freedom from curious eyes. After moving the table, I came inside the trailer and gathered my wrapping supplies, made sure the kids were occupied, and marched back into the house to begin my holiday work. I was in there for about an hour, when it dawned on me that I was actually wrapping presents in my own home—in my empty, wall-less, bare, cold, unprotected, Christmas tree-less, no smell of cookies, fire-in-the-fireplace-less, holiday music-less, broken, bruised home. But what was neat was that I was okay.

I felt a peace I can't explain and I truly enjoyed standing in there in the cold wrapping presents for my family and friends. It was okay. I wasn't bitter, I wasn't resentful, I wasn't angry, I wasn't wishing I were somewhere else. I was exactly where I wanted to be and better yet, I felt I was where I should be. It was strange, but in a really good way.

I hope that what I experienced tonight is how you feel about OLG and Bay St. Louis. I hope that even though you are surrounded by loss and devastation, that even though you are being pulled into a million different directions, that even though the work you are faced with seems too much for one human being, that despite all that, you feel that you are where you want to be and better yet, that you feel you are exactly where you should be.

I am sure this is not how you intended to spend the final years of your career as a diocesan priest and I know it is not how I wanted to spend any portion of my life, but I admire and appreciate you and how you are handling what has happened because you have set an example for me. You don't complain, you don't hide, and you don't make life miserable for those around you. You do what needs to be done, you try to keep a positive attitude, you use your sense of humor—you shine. Not for one minute do I pretend it is easy for you because I know otherwise. It breaks my heart that this has been laid at your doorstep and I feel the same for all the other priests who are in the same boat. But at the same time, I am forever grateful that you are here because, like wrapping Christmas presents in a cold, gutted house, it feel peaceful.

Thank you for all that you do. Thank you for being who you are and for sharing your gifts with us. I feel so privileged to know you. You look out for me and my family and I appreciate that. You mean so much to so many people. You are simply a very special person.

A long road lies ahead for all of us but I am grateful that you are in our lives to travel it with us.

When I count the blessings in my life, you are one of them.

God bless you and may your Christmas and New Year be peaceful and filled with love.

Sincerely,
Jo.

On August 29, 2005, the church sign in Bay St. Louis, Mississippi, reads, "It is when you loose everything that you are free to do anything." Little does it anticipate the fury of Hurricane Katrina which arrives early that same morning. Yes! She was no lady!

Many words have been used to describe her. Many stories have been told about her. Many curses have been expressed about it. Many tears have been shed over her. Many a heart has been broken because of her. Many a despairing moment has been lived because of her. Many a lonely moment has filled with doubt because of her. Many a weary spirit has been conquered by her. Many a memory has been stolen because of her. Many a friend has been lost because of her. Many a bottle of water has been drunk because of her. Many a question has been asked because of her. Many a family has been torn apart because of her. Many a MRE has been eaten because of her. Many a portable toilet has been visited because of her. Many a dream has been shattered because of her. Many a shoulder has been leaned upon because of her. Many a silence has been created because of her. Many a future has become a past tense.

Her maiden name was "Cleansing." It was very appropriate. Why did she have to be so thorough? Why did she have to dish out such a deadly blow? Why was she so aggressive? Why was she so indiscriminate? Why was she so controlling? Where was her mercy instead of her fury? Where was her feminine quality? Was she sent to do the Lord's bidding? Why could she not have been gentler and kinder? Why do we need such a drastic warning? Why do we have to have such a 'wake up call'? Why did she have to traumatize so many people? Why did she add to the homeless population? Why did she have to challenge our sincerity? Our values? Our priorities? Our hopes? Why did she have to be in control? Why did she have to bring out the worst and best in people? Why didn't she choose other less dramatic ways of doing it? Why was she so odiferous? Why did she disturb our tranquility? Why did she devastate our landscapes and the landscapes of our lives? Why did she turn the lives of so many people upside down and inside out? Why do all the questions she forces us to ask ourselves lead to deeper questions that have no easy answers?

Yet, amid all the "whys," there are by-products that otherwise we might have never known. Why are people so genuine and caring now? Why do we stop and talk without thoughts of time or deadlines? Why do people hug each other genuinely? Why do strangers show up on people's doorsteps and lend a helping hand? Why do people line up in the heat of the day for hours to get a hot meal and still not complain? Why does the "God bless you" seem more genuine now? Why do people say that they will be praying for you and it won't be an empty gesture? Why do people say "It is good to see you" and really mean it? Why do people not tire listening to each other's survival story without complaining? Why do even seemingly emotionless and independent reporters shed a tear even in public? Why do people open their hearts and homes to complete strangers? Why are people so open and trusting at such a time? Why do people get up again and again after such a horrific experience? Why do people say over and over again, "Is there anything I can do for you?" Why do people ask, "How are you doing?" and genuinely mean it? Why do people stop rushing around at breakneck speed and instead even drive below the posted speed limit? Why do people communicate more face to face now than through the technological gismos? Why are people more humble and accepting now? Why are people more at peace now in their skin even if they have to accept hand-me-downs from someone else?

Yes, there are a lot of "whys" and I think all of us will continue to ask "why" and in the asking discover an answer that, in the past was hidden in the rubble of our lives but now such rubble has been "cleansed" and we can see it more clearly.

Maybe, she wasn't a lady. But, then again, maybe we needed to meet her and marry her to discover the answer to all our "whys."

978-0-595-39079-3
0-595-39079-X

Printed in the United States
50886LVS00004B/29